Table of Contents

The Company's Coming Story

Jean Paré grew up understanding that the combination of family, friends and home cooking is the essence of a good life. From her mother she learned to appreciate good cooking, while her father praised even her earliest attempts. When she left home she took with her many acquired family recipes, a love of cooking and an intriguing desire to read recipe books like novels!

"never share a recipe you wouldn't use yourself"

In 1963, when her four children had all reached school age, Jean volunteered to cater the 50th anniversary of the Vermilion School of Agriculture, now Lakeland College. Working out of her home, Jean prepared a dinner for over 1000 people which launched a flourishing catering operation that continued for over eighteen years. During that time she was provided with countless opportunities to test new ideas with immediate feedback—resulting in empty plates and contented customers! Whether preparing cocktail sandwiches for a house party or serving a hot meal for 1500 people, Jean Paré earned a reputation for good food, courteous service and reasonable prices.

"Why don't you write a cookbook?" Time and again, as requests for her recipes mounted, Jean was asked that question. Jean's response was to team up with her son, Grant Lovig, in the fall of 1980 to form Company's Coming Publishing Limited. April 14, 1981, marked the debut of "150 DELICIOUS SQUARES", the first Company's Coming cookbook in what soon would become Canada's most popular cookbook series.

Jean Paré's operation has grown steadily from the early days of working out of a spare bedroom in her home. Full-time staff includes marketing personnel located in major cities across Canada. Home Office is based in Edmonton, Alberta in a modern building constructed specially for the company.

Today the company distributes throughout Canada and the United States in addition to numerous overseas markets, all under the guidance of Jean's daughter, Gail Lovig. Best-sellers many times over, Company's Coming cookbooks are published in English and French, plus a Spanish-language edition is available in Mexico. Familiar and trusted in home kitchens the world over, Company's Coming cookbooks are offered in a variety of formats, including the original softcover series.

Jean Paré's approach to cooking has always called for quick and easy recipes using everyday ingredients. Even when traveling, she is constantly on the lookout for new ideas to share with her readers. At home, she can usually be found researching and  writing recipes, or working in the company's test kitchen. Jean continues to gain new supporters by adhering to what she calls "the golden rule of cooking": never share a recipe you wouldn't use yourself. It's an approach that works—*millions of times over!*

Foreword

What's your definition of a make-ahead meal? An entire meal in the freezer ready to reheat and serve? Or a few things done ahead of time so final meal preparation is quicker and easier? Whatever your definition, the recipes in this cookbook will make mealtimes more about eating great food and less about rushing to prepare them.

Each Make-Ahead Meals recipe has a footnote so you can see at a glance the advance preparation time needed and the make-ahead/freeze-ahead possibilities. Some recipes are fully cooked, ready and waiting in the freezer; others can be started ahead of time, needing only final touches at the last minute. Although most recipes in this cookbook can be served immediately, they're designed to be made ahead.

The Progressive Recipes section has a Base Recipe that can be made, stored and then used to prepare a variety of different dishes. These include main course meals, breads and desserts.

To take full advantage of *Make-Ahead Meals*, check out Plan Ahead and Freezer Storage on pages 8 through 11.

And for busy weeknights, Select-A-Meal (see pages 12 and 13) is the perfect answer to staying relaxed about meal preparation. Team up the meat, vegetables and starch of your choice from the freezer, with a make-ahead salad chilling in the refrigerator, and a good part of the work is

already done. In just a short time, you'll have a balanced meal ready to serve!

Make-Ahead Meals offers more than 120 kitchen-tested recipes that will save you time—try them and see for yourself!

Jean Paré

Each recipe has been analyzed using the most up-to-date version of the Canadian Nutrient File from Health Canada, which is based upon the United States Department of Agriculture (USDA) Nutrient Data Base.

Margaret Ng, B.Sc. (Hon), M.A.
Registered Dietician

plan ahead

The secret to make-ahead meals is to plan ahead. Here's a list of tips to help you get started—sooner!

1. Shop smart. Write out complete menus for the upcoming week and create your shopping list based on those menus. Check staples before you go to the grocery store to eliminate extra trips. Remember: A smart list results in a shopping trip that is more productive and cost-effective.

2. Get ready, get set. The best time to get a jump on meal preparation is when you come home with the week's groceries:

   - Wash salad greens, remove excess water, then refrigerate in sealable plastic bags.

   - Divide fresh meat into appropriate serving sizes, then wrap, label and freeze.

   - Chop or slice vegetables and store in sealable plastic bags to make stir-fry during the week a cinch. See Marinated Beef Strips, page 38; Marinated Chicken Strips, page 40; and Precut Veggies, page 39, for additional ideas.

3. Double up and halve your time. Double a recipe, freeze half and you've got a made-ahead meal ready and waiting, without double the work.

4. Cook and share. Spend a day with a friend or several neighbors cooking larger quantities of several recipes. Have a great time visiting—and fill several freezers while you're at it!

For many busy households, weekends are the time to do the bulk of timesaving work. Here are several other ways to get an upper hand on suppertime:

5. Prepare a salad dressing in the morning, and flavors will blend nicely during the day.

6. Brown ground beef, onions and seasonings the night before.

7. Set the table before you head off to work.

8. Peel carrots and potatoes in the morning. Leave whole, cover with cold water and refrigerate until ready to cook. Cut up the vegetables and change the water just before cooking.

9. Read Storage Tips, page 9; Freezer Storage, pages 10 and 11; and Select-A-Meal, pages 12 and 13.

Whatever way you decide to plan ahead, you and your family will benefit with less stress at mealtime and more time for each other!

storage tips

With proper storage, you can preserve the flavor, appearance, texture, and nutrition of all your make-ahead recipes. Follow our guidelines for storing, refrigerating, freezing and thawing food, and you'll be serving good quality food every time.

1. Whether you're storing food in a cupboard, refrigerator or freezer, start by wrapping the food correctly to seal out air and seal in flavor and moisture. For best results, choose:

   • rigid containers made of plastic, glass, metal, or heavily waxed cardboard, with lids that form a tight seal; or

   • flexible wrappings such as heavy foil, clear plastic wrap and bags, and laminated paper; fold the edges together for an air-tight seal.

2. When choosing the wrapping material, consider what will be done with the food when it's taken out of the freezer. If a cake is to be warmed before serving, wrap it in foil. Put your casserole mixture in a freezer-to-oven dish so it can be frozen, thawed and reheated in the same container.

3. Wrap and chill or freeze foods as soon as possible after cooking. Large volumes of hot food that might raise the internal temperature of your fridge or freezer, or dishes that are too hot to wrap, can be cooled quickly by placing the dish in ice-cold water. For food safety, avoid cooling foods at room temperature.

◆ **Shelf Storage**

Store staples such as flour, sugar and canned goods in a cool, dry, well-ventilated place, away from sunlight. The best storage temperature is 50 to 70°F (10 to 21.1°C).

◆ **Refrigerator Storage**

Keep refrigerator temperature at about 40°F (4.4°C). Check periodically with an appliance thermometer.

◆ **Freezer Storage**

Keep freezer temperature at 0°F (-18°C) or less. Check periodically with an appliance thermometer.

freezer storage

♦ **Recommendations for freezing**

Appetizers: 1 to 2 months

Breads: Bake breads before freezing—dough that has been thawed and baked after freezing will produce a smaller, tougher loaf. Overwrap bread you buy if it's to stay in the freezer for more than one week.
> *Quick Breads:* 2 to 3 months
> *Yeast Breads:* 9 months

Cakes: Freeze frosted cakes without wrapping, but wrap as soon as they're firm. To prevent crushing, place cake in a box, then overwrap box. Icing (confectioner's) sugar icings and fudge frostings freeze particularly well.
> *Frosted:* 1 to 2 months
> *Unfrosted:* 4 to 6 months
> *Casseroles:* 2 to 3 months

Cookies: Most baked cookies can be frozen. Freeze frosted cookies, uncovered, until they are firm, then wrap.
> *Frosted:* 2 to 3 months
> *Unfrosted:* 9 to 12 months

Fruits and Vegetables: Freeze at the peak of their ripeness. Peeled fruit that discolors easily, such as apples and pears, should be dipped in a lemon juice solution (3 tbsp., 50 mL lemon juice to 2 cups, 500 mL water) before freezing. Berries can be frozen, uncovered, on a tray until firm, then transferred to an air-tight container for freezer storage. If the fruit is to be used as pie filling, layer it with sugar (only fruit that doesn't discolor is suitable for this method of freezing).
> *Citrus Fruits:* 3 to 4 months
> *Other Fruits:* 1 year
> *Vegetables:* 1 year

Main Dishes: Bake until almost done, then freeze; dish will finish cooking during reheating.

Meat, Poultry, Fish: Freeze fresh product as promptly as possible. Cooked meat in a sauce and leftover roasts freeze very well; they should be slightly undercooked before freezing as they will finish cooking during reheating.

Pies and Pastry: To prevent soggy crusts, bake pies before freezing.
> *Chiffon Pies:* 1 month
> *Other Pies:* 4 months
> *Pastry:* 4 months

Sandwiches: Most sandwiches freeze very well but not for longer than about 1 month. If you freeze make-ahead sandwiches for lunch boxes, rotate them so that the oldest get used first. Put them directly from freezer to lunch box; they'll be defrosted by lunchtime and, at the same time, will keep other items in the box cold.

Soups: Leave headspace in the containers to allow for expansion of the frozen liquid. For quicker reheating, package soups in reasonably small portions; the larger the block of frozen soup, the longer it takes to reheat it.

♦ **Freezer do's and don'ts**

1. *The Golden Rule:* The better the quality of the food that goes into the freezer—the better the quality that comes out!

2. *Keep cool:* Your freezer should be at a constant temperature of 0°F (-18°C). If you don't have a frost-free model, it should be defrosted every 6 to 12 months, depending on how often you open and close the lid and how much empty space there is.

3. *Frost-free zone:* If you find that your freezer is less than half full most of the time, place an empty, sturdy cardboard box upside down on the

bottom of the freezer to use up frost-building space.

4. *Checklist:* Keep a notebook next to the freezer, or tape a sheet of paper to the lid, to record food items and dates frozen; stroke off items as they are used. To ensure best quality product, use frozen food within the recommended period of time. An accurate inventory record will also help you plan major shopping trips.

5. *Containers:* Suitable containers for freezing include: plastic containers with airtight lids, aluminum foil containers with lids and plastic sealable freezer bags. Regardless of the packaging, remove as much of the air as possible before sealing. If you freeze food in a covered casserole dish, use masking tape around the lid to make an air-tight seal. With rigid containers, leave about $1/4$ to 1 inch (6 mm to 2.5 cm) at the top to allow for expansion of the food as it freezes.

6. *Label:* Use a permanent marker or self-adhesive labels to label everything. Include the name of the item, the date it was put into the freezer and any final cooking instructions—it's no good knowing how long something can be stored if you don't know the date you froze it.

7. *Cooldown:* Chill foods before they go into the freezer. This can be done before or after packaging.

8. *Together but apart:* Waxed or baking paper is great for separating layers or items such as crêpes, fish fillets and pork chops, so that you can defrost individual portions rather than the whole batch.

9. *Easy Removal:* To freeze soups and stews: line a bowl with a plastic bag, pour the soup or stew into the bag, seal it and place the bowl in the freezer. Once frozen, remove the bag and store it on its own.

Foods that do not freeze well:
- hard-boiled eggs go rubbery
- fried and crumbed meats become soggy
- whole eggs in their shells will break the shell as they expand
- vegetables with a high water content spoil
- sour cream and yogurt separate
- meringues weep
- herbs and spices lose their flavor after about 2 weeks
- custards, mayonnaise and dishes containing gelatin won't, in fact, freeze at all

What is "freezer burn?"

The primary purpose of freezer packaging is to exclude air from the food, although it also serves to keep the food clean and sanitary, and to separate different kinds of foods. The air in freezers is dry because moisture is frozen and deposited on walls and freezing coils. Improperly packaged foods allow the dry air in the freezer to extract moisture from the frozen foods, resulting in "freezer burn." Dry, discolored spots are the tip-off that freezer burn has occurred. While the quality of the food is lowered in both taste and texture, it doesn't indicate spoilage.

select-a-meal

Deciding what's for dinner just got easier! A freezer full of ready-made dishes means you only have to make choices—not recipes—to create a meal. And to make choosing really easy, organize your freezer by category so you don't have to shift and move all sorts of containers to find what you're looking for. A section for meats and separate ones for vegetables, starches and breads is a good starting point. Color-coding containers with tape or permanent marker also works for easy visual reference.

You may want to freeze these recipes in individual portions, but they won't keep as long as larger portions so be prepared to use them within two weeks to a month.

With Select-A-Meal, the variety of combinations is endless and certainly not limited to the recipes in this cookbook. Try freezing your own recipes in quantities suitable for your family. Or create a complete meal on a freezer plate for single-serving reheating. The economy of preparing meals at home always makes sense.

Listed below and on page 13, are recipes which we feel best fit into the Select-A-Meal category. They are listed by food group for easy meal planning.

◆ Breads ◆

Cheese And Onion Muffins, page 56
Corn And Pepper Pancakes, page 57
Freezer Biscuits, page 76
Seed And Cheese Wedges, page 59
Surprise Corn Bread, page 58

◆ Cookies ◆

Chewy Chocolate Cookies, page 84
Chocolate Cinnamon Cookies, page 87
Peanut Butter Cookies, page 85

◆ Desserts ◆

Apple Coffee Cake, page 62
Dried Fruit Cheese Cake, page 97
Gingerbread Cake, page 63
Poppy Seed Cake, page 91

♦ Main Dishes ♦

♦ Sauces for Meatballs and Patties ♦

♦ Starches ♦

♦ Vegetables/Egg Dishes ♦

Progressive recipes

Progressive recipes
This special section features Base Recipes that can be frozen and later combined with additional ingredients to "progress" to the final recipe. The introduction of each recipe provides a list of other recipes that can be made from it, but don't let these suggestions limit you. The possibilities for the Marinated Beef Strips, page 38, for example, are as endless as your imagination.

Make-Ahead Roast And Gravy

(BASE RECIPE)

Use in Stacked Beef Dip, page 15, or to have roast and gravy on hand for the family while the cook's away.

Top sirloin beef roast	4 lbs.	1.8 kg
Water	½ cup	125 mL
GRAVY		
Beef drippings, plus water to make	4 cups	1 L
All-purpose flour	½ cup	125 mL
Salt	1 tsp.	5 mL
Pepper	¼ tsp.	1 mL
Water	1 cup	250 mL
Liquid gravy browner (optional, for color)		

Place roast in medium roasting pan. Add water. Cover. Roast in 300°F (150°C) oven for about 1½ hours until medium rare to medium or to desired doneness. Pour drippings and any brown bits into small container. Makes about 2 cups (500 mL) drippings. Chill drippings and roast separately. Remove and discard any hardened fat on drippings. Thinly slice cooled roast across the grain.

(continued on next page)

Gravy: Heat beef drippings and water in large saucepan until boiling.

Stir flour, salt and pepper in small bowl. Mix in water until smooth. Stir into drippings until boiling and thickened. Add gravy browner. Makes 5 cups (1.25 L) gravy. Makes 16 servings, enough for 4 packages of roast and 4 containers of gravy.

1 serving: 152 Calories; 4.3 g Total Fat; 259 mg Sodium; 23 g Protein; 3 g Carbohydrate; trace Dietary Fiber

---

Make Ahead And Freeze: Divide cooked beef slices among 4 sealable freezer bags (4 servings in each). Remove air, seal and label. Freeze for up to 3 months. Divide gravy among 4 freezer containers (4 servings each). Label. Freeze for up to 3 months. To serve, heat 1 portion of gravy in large saucepan, adding a bit of water to thin to desired consistency. Add 1 package thawed beef. Cover. Heat on medium-low until hot.

Select-A-Meal: See page 12.

Stacked Beef Dip

Spread buns with a little prepared horseradish or mustard for some zip!

◆ Base Recipe: package of Make-Ahead Roast, page 14	1	1
Can of condensed beef broth	10 oz.	284 mL
Water	1 cup	250 mL
Mini submarine buns, split	4	4

Base Recipe: Thaw package of Make-Ahead Roast.

Heat beef broth and water in large saucepan. Add roast beef. Cover. Simmer for 20 minutes until very tender.

Toast buns under broiler. Remove beef, using slotted spoon, and divide among bottom halves of buns. Cover with bun tops. Ladle broth into individual bowls for dipping. Makes 4 sandwiches.

1 sandwich (with dip): 370 Calories; 8.8 g Total Fat; 901 mg Sodium; 31 g Protein; 40 g Carbohydrate; 2 g Dietary Fiber

Stewed Beef

(BASE RECIPE)

What a perfect way to have tender beef available.
Use in Beef Stew And Vegetables, page 19.

Stew beef	4 lbs.	1.8 kg
Water, to cover		
Medium onions, chopped	4	4
Salt	1 tbsp.	15 mL
Pepper	1 tsp.	5 mL
Liquid gravy browner (optional, for color)		
Water	½ cup	125 mL
All-purpose flour	¼ cup	60 mL

Cut beef into smaller cubes. Simmer beef cubes and water in large saucepan for 1½ hours. Skim off foam as necessary. Add more water, as needed, to keep beef covered. Beef should be tender.

Add onion, salt, pepper and gravy browner. Simmer for about 30 minutes until beef is very tender and onion is soft.

Stir water and flour in small bowl until smooth. Stir into beef mixture until boiling and thickened. Cool. Makes 8 cups (2 L), enough for 4 containers.

½ cup (125 mL): 126 Calories; 3.5 g Total Fat; 473 mg Sodium; 18 g Protein; 4 g Carbohydrate; 1 g Dietary Fiber

Make Ahead And Freeze: Divide beef mixture among four 2½ cup (625 mL) freezer containers. Label. Freeze for up to 3 months.

Select-A-Meal: See page 12.

1. Oriental Bean Salad, page 122
2. Squash And Beef Pie, page 21
3. Freezer Biscuits, page 76

Props Courtesy Of: Stokes
The Bay
X/S Wares

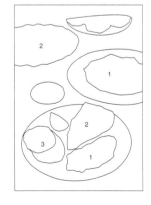

Beef Stew And Vegetables

A taste of home cooking like you remember.

◆ Base Recipe: container of Stewed Beef, page 16	1	1
Sliced carrot, cut into ½ inch (12 mm) pieces	1½ cups	375 mL
Potato, cut into 1 inch (2.5 cm) cubes	2 cups	500 mL
Celery ribs, cut into 1 inch (2.5 cm) pieces	2	2
Chopped onion	⅔ cup	150 mL

Base Recipe: Thaw container of Stewed Beef.

Empty stewed beef into 3 quart (3 L) casserole. Add carrot, potato, celery and onion. Stir. Cover. Bake in 325°F (160°C) oven for 1 hour until vegetables are tender. Makes 6½ cups (1.6 L). Serves 4.

1 serving: 221 Calories; 3.7 g Total Fat; 584 mg Sodium; 21 g Protein; 26 g Carbohydrate; 4 g Dietary Fiber

Variation: To speed up cooking, this recipe may also be cooked in large saucepan with 1 cup (250 mL) water until vegetables are tender.

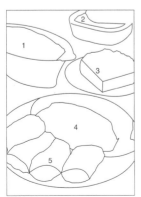

1. Quick Chili, page 27
2. Seasoned Beef And Onions, page 20
3. Shepherd's Pie, page 22
4. Beefy Salad, page 24
5. Beefy Salad Wraps, page 24

Props Courtesy Of: Chintz & Company

Seasoned Beef And Onions

(BASE RECIPE)

Can be made in four batches on the stovetop, or in an electric frying pan. Handy to have in the freezer for Squash And Beef Pie, page 21; Shepherd's Pie, page 22; Potato-Topped Casserole, page 23; Beefy Salad, page 24; Sloppy Joes, page 25; Meaty Bean Bake, page 26; or Quick Chili, page 27.

Lean ground beef	8 lbs.	3.6 kg
Chopped onion	6 cups	1.5 L
Garlic cloves, minced (or 1½ tsp., 7 mL, powder)	6	6
Cooking oil	2 tbsp.	30 mL
Seasoned salt	2 tbsp.	30 mL
Freshly ground pepper	2 tsp.	10 mL

Measure ¼ of ground beef, ¼ of onion, ¼ of garlic and ¼ of cooking oil into large frying pan. Sprinkle with ¼ of seasoned salt and ¼ of pepper. Scramble-fry for about 10 minutes until no pink remains in beef. Place in large colander to drain. Repeat, in three equal batches, with remaining ingredients. Combine with first batch of beef mixture in large bowl or roaster. Cool. Makes 21 cups (5.25 L), enough for 7 packages.

1 cup (250 mL): 288 Calories; 15.1 g Total Fat; 399 mg Sodium; 32 g Protein; 5 g Carbohydrate; 1 g Dietary Fiber

Pictured on page 18.

Make Ahead And Freeze: Divide beef mixture among seven 3 cup (750 mL) freezer containers or sealable plastic freezer bags. Label. Freeze for up to 3 months.

Paré Pointer

The sign said, "No standing anytime," so he sat down on the curb.

Squash And Beef Pie

Bright orange butternut squash covers a beef and mushroom base—a new twist to Shepherd's Pie. Has a hint-of-sweetness flavor. Uses Sweetened Butternut Squash, page 148. A very tasty dish.

◆ Base Recipe: package of Seasoned Beef And Onions, page 20	1	1
Margarine (or butter)	2 tbsp.	30 mL
Chopped fresh mushrooms	1 cup	250 mL
All-purpose flour	1 tbsp.	15 mL
Pepper, sprinkle		
Water	½ cup	125 mL
Beef bouillon powder	1 tsp.	5 mL
Dried thyme	½ tsp.	2 mL
Packages of Sweetened Butternut Squash, page 148, thawed (about 4 cups, 1 L)	2	2
Large egg, fork-beaten	1	1
Paprika, sprinkle		
Margarine (or butter), melted (optional)		

Base Recipe: Thaw package of Seasoned Beef And Onions.

Melt margarine in large frying pan. Add mushrooms. Heat on medium, stirring occasionally, until liquid has evaporated and mushrooms are golden.

Sprinkle with flour and pepper. Stir well. Slowly add water, stirring continually, until boiling and thickened. Sprinkle with bouillon powder and thyme. Stir. Add beef and onion mixture. Stir. Pack in bottom of greased 10 inch (25 cm) pie plate or 9 inch (22 cm) deep-dish pie plate.

Stir squash and egg in medium bowl. Spread or pipe over beef mixture. Sprinkle with paprika. If desired, brush melted margarine on squash layer before baking. Bake, uncovered, in 350°F (175°C) oven for 30 to 35 minutes until heated through. Serves 6.

1 serving: 267 Calories; 13.1 g Total Fat; 472 mg Sodium; 20 g Protein; 20 g Carbohydrate; 4 g Dietary Fiber

Pictured on page 17.

To Make Ahead: Assemble early in day or night before. To serve, bake as above.

Shepherd's Pie

This is the more traditional recipe but with a make-ahead twist.
The mixture of potato and turnip is also a slight variation.

◆ Base Recipe: package of Seasoned Beef And Onions, page 20	1	1
Medium potatoes, cut up	2	2
Medium yellow turnip, peeled and cut up a bit smaller than potato	1	1
Water		
Margarine (or butter)	1 tbsp.	15 mL
Salt	½ tsp.	2 mL
Pepper	⅛ tsp.	0.5 mL
Can of condensed cream of mushroom soup	10 oz.	284 mL
All-purpose flour	1 tbsp.	15 mL
Can of kernel corn (or 1½ cups, 375 mL, frozen corn, cooked), drained	12 oz.	341 mL
Frozen peas, cooked and drained	1 cup	250 mL
Ketchup	1½ tbsp.	25 mL
Prepared horseradish	1 tsp.	5 mL
Beef bouillon powder	2 tsp.	10 mL
Pepper	¼ tsp.	1 mL
Worcestershire sauce	1 tsp.	5 mL
Paprika, sprinkle		

Base Recipe: Thaw package of Seasoned Beef And Onions.

Boil potato and turnip in water in large covered saucepan for 20 minutes until turnip is tender. Drain cooking liquid, reserving ¼ cup (60 mL).

Mash, adding reserved liquid, margarine, salt and pepper, until quite smooth. Set aside.

Combine next 9 ingredients in large bowl. Add beef and onion mixture. Mix well. Pack evenly into ungreased 8 x 8 inch (20 x 20 cm) pan.

(continued on next page)

Spread mashed potato mixture on top. Sprinkle with paprika. Cover with foil. Bake in 350°F (175°C) oven for 45 minutes. Remove foil. Bake for 10 to 15 minutes until potato is crusty and golden. Serves 4.

1 serving: 478 Calories; 21.3 g Total Fat; 1852 mg Sodium; 31 g Protein; 42 g Carbohydrate; 6 g Dietary Fiber

Pictured on page 18.

To Make Ahead: Assemble early in day or night before. Cover. Chill. To serve, bake as above.

Potato-Topped Casserole

This is a warm, comfortable casserole—similar to Shepherd's Pie. Very quick and easy.

◆ Base Recipe: package of Seasoned Beef And Onions, page 20	1	1
Can of condensed tomato soup	10 oz.	284 mL
Can of cream-style corn	14 oz.	398 mL
Salt	½ tsp.	2 mL
Pepper	¼ tsp.	1 mL
Parsley flakes	1 tsp.	5 mL
Mashed potato	3 cups	750 mL
Grated medium Cheddar cheese (optional)	1 cup	250 mL

Base Recipe: Thaw package of Seasoned Beef And Onions.

Combine beef and onion mixture, soup, corn, salt, pepper and parsley in large bowl. Mix well. Turn into ungreased 2 quart (2 L) casserole.

Spread potato over top. Sprinkle with cheese. Bake, uncovered, in 350°F (175°C) oven for 35 minutes until heated through and cheese is melted. Serves 4.

1 serving: 526 Calories; 20.4 g Total Fat; 1956 mg Sodium; 30 g Protein; 61 g Carbohydrate; 6 g Dietary Fiber

To Make Ahead: Assemble early in day or night before. Cover. Chill. To serve, bake as above.

Beefy Salad

A full-meal salad.

◆ Base Recipe: package of Seasoned Beef And Onions, page 20	1	1
Water	2 cups	500 mL
Salt	½ tsp.	2 mL
Brown rice	1 cup	250 mL
Can of red kidney beans, drained	14 oz.	398 mL
Chunky salsa	1½ cups	375 mL
Chili powder	¾ tsp.	4 mL
Granulated sugar	½ tsp.	2 mL
Salt	½ tsp.	2 mL
Pepper	¼ tsp.	1 mL
Ground cumin	¼ tsp.	1 mL
Shredded iceberg lettuce	6 cups	1.5 L
Grated light sharp Cheddar cheese	¾ cup	175 mL

Base Recipe: Thaw package of Seasoned Beef And Onions.

Bring water and salt to a boil in medium saucepan. Stir in rice. Cover. Simmer for about 45 minutes until rice is tender and moisture is absorbed.

Combine next 7 ingredients in large non-stick frying pan. Add beef and onion mixture. Heat on medium, stirring frequently, until hot. Combine with cooked rice.

Divide lettuce among 6 individual plates. Spoon beef mixture onto lettuce. Top each with 2 tbsp. (30 mL) cheese. Serves 8.

1 serving: 304 Calories; 9.1 g Total Fat; 1363 mg Sodium; 21 g Protein; 35 g Carbohydrate; 5 g Dietary Fiber

Pictured on page 18.

To Make Ahead: Early in day, cook rice as described and mix with next 7 ingredients. Chill. To serve, reheat and proceed to finish salad.

BEEFY SALAD WRAPS: Divide beef and rice mixture among 8 warmed 10 inch (25 cm) flour tortillas. Top each with 2 tbsp. (30 mL) cheese. Microwave on high (100%) for 30 seconds. Add about ¼ cup (60 mL) lettuce to each. Top with salsa and dollop of sour cream. Fold in opposite sides and roll tightly to enclose filling. Cut in half crosswise to serve. Makes 8 wraps.

Sloppy Joes

A quick and easy supper to serve over toasted buns. Thick and rich-tasting.

◆ Base Recipe: package of Seasoned Beef And Onions, page 20	1	1
Water	½ cup	125 mL
Chili sauce	½ cup	125 mL
Can of tomato sauce	7½ oz.	213 mL
Brown sugar, packed	1 tbsp.	15 mL
Worcestershire sauce	1½ tsp.	7 mL
Lemon juice	1 tsp.	5 mL
Salt, sprinkle		
Pepper, sprinkle		
Milk	⅓ cup	75 mL
All-purpose flour	2 tbsp.	30 mL

Base Recipe: Thaw package of Seasoned Beef And Onions.

Empty beef and onion mixture into large saucepan. Add next 8 ingredients. Heat, stirring occasionally, until boiling. Simmer for 8 minutes.

Stir milk and flour in cup until smooth. Add to beef mixture. Heat, stirring continually, until boiling and thickened. Makes 4 cups (1 L). Serves 4.

1 serving: 312 Calories; 12.2 g Total Fat; 1144 mg Sodium; 27 g Protein; 24 g Carbohydrate; 4 g Dietary Fiber

To Make Ahead: Assemble and prepare early in day or night before. Cover. Chill. To serve, reheat.

Paré Pointer

The big candle told the little candle that it was too young to go out.

Meaty Bean Bake

Looks as good as it tastes! Hearty, stick-to-the-ribs food!

◆ Base Recipe: package of Seasoned Beef And Onions, page 20	1	1
Can of kidney beans, with liquid	14 oz.	398 mL
Can of beans in tomato sauce	14 oz.	398 mL
Can of lima beans, drained	14 oz.	398 mL
Can of garbanzo beans (chick peas), drained	14 oz.	398 mL
Barbecue sauce	⅓ cup	75 mL
Picante salsa	½ cup	125 mL
Fancy (mild) molasses	2 tbsp.	30 mL
Brown sugar, packed	⅓ cup	75 mL
Worcestershire sauce	1½ tsp.	7 mL
Prepared mustard	2 tsp.	10 mL

Base Recipe: Thaw package of Seasoned Beef And Onions.

Empty beef and onion mixture into large bowl. Add remaining
10 ingredients. Mix well. Turn into ungreased 2½ quart (2.5 L) casserole.
Bake, uncovered, in 350°F (175°C) oven for 40 to 45 minutes until bubbly
and browned around edge. Stir partway through so beans on top do not
dry out. Makes 9 cups (2.25 L). Serves 8.

*1 serving: 348 Calories; 7.3 g Total Fat; 1046 mg Sodium; 23 g Protein; 50 g Carbohydrate;
12 g Dietary Fiber*

To Make Ahead: Assemble early in day or night before. Cover. Chill. To
serve, bake as above.

tip   *When cooking frozen meat mixtures, stir frequently to speed up
thawing, but gently to avoid breaking up food.*

Quick Chili

Combine this all in mere minutes and then simmer briefly. Spiced just right.

◆ Base Recipe: package of Seasoned Beef And Onions, page 20	1	1
Can of diced tomatoes, with juice	14 oz.	398 mL
Can of stewed tomatoes, with juice, chopped	14 oz.	398 mL
Cans of kidney beans (14 oz., 398 mL, each), drained	2	2
Can of diced green chilies, with liquid	4 oz.	114 mL
Chili powder	2 tsp.	10 mL
Granulated sugar	1 tsp.	5 mL
Dried whole oregano	2 tsp.	10 mL
Salt	1 tsp.	5 mL
Freshly ground pepper	½ tsp.	2 mL

Base Recipe: Thaw package of Seasoned Beef And Onions.

Empty beef and onion mixture into large saucepan. Add remaining 9 ingredients. Heat, stirring often, until hot and bubbling. Makes 8 cups (2 L). Serves 6.

1 serving: 286 Calories; 8.7 g Total Fat; 1348 mg Sodium; 24 g Protein; 30 g Carbohydrate; 8 g Dietary Fiber

Pictured on page 18.

To Make Ahead: Assemble and prepare early in day or night before. Cover. Chill. To serve, reheat.

Paré Pointer

You wouldn't starve in a desert. Just eat the sand-which is there.

Meatballs

(BASE RECIPE)

*Mild in flavor. Use with any of the sauces
that follow on pages 31 to 37.*

Large eggs, fork-beaten	4	4
Milk	1 cup	250 mL
Finely chopped onion	½ cup	125 mL
Dry bread crumbs	2 cups	500 mL
Worcestershire sauce	4 tsp.	20 mL
Salt	4 tsp.	20 mL
Pepper	1 tsp.	5 mL
Lean ground beef	4 lbs.	1.8 kg

Combine eggs, milk, onion, bread crumbs, Worcestershire sauce, salt and pepper in large bowl. Stir until well blended.

Mix in ground beef. Shape into 1½ inch (3.8 cm) balls. Arrange on greased baking sheet. Bake in 425°F (220°C) oven for 15 to 16 minutes until no pink remains. Drain. Makes about 8 dozen (96) meatballs.

6 meatballs: 257 Calories; 11.5 g Total Fat; 866 mg Sodium; 24 g Protein; 12 g Carbohydrate; trace Dietary Fiber

Make Ahead And Freeze: Place baked meatballs in single layer on baking sheet. Freeze 2 hours then remove to freezer bag. Label. Freeze for up to 3 months. To serve from frozen state, see Tip, page 30.

Select-A-Meal: See page 12.

For uniform meatballs; 1. use a scoop (looks like a miniature ice-cream scoop and is available at hotel and restaurant supply stores in a variety of sizes), 2. press beef mixture into a square or rectangle shape, same thickness all over. Cut into smaller squares. Roll each square into a ball.

Breaded Meatballs

(BASE RECIPE)

Crispy on the outside. Use with any
of the sauces that follow on pages 31 to 37.

Large eggs, fork-beaten	4	4
Fine dry bread crumbs	2 cups	500 mL
Dill weed	4 tsp.	20 mL
Seasoned salt	1 tsp.	5 mL
Salt	1 tsp.	5 mL
Pepper	½ tsp.	2 mL
Liquid gravy browner	1 tsp.	5 mL
Lean ground beef	2 lbs.	900 g
Ground chicken	2 lbs.	900 g
Large eggs, fork-beaten	4	4
Water	¼ cup	60 mL
Fine dry bread crumbs	1⅓ cups	325 mL

Stir first 7 ingredients in medium bowl.

Mix in ground beef and chicken. Shape into 1½ inch (3.8 cm) balls, rolling in palms of hands.

Mix second amount of eggs and water in small bowl until smooth.

Measure second amount of bread crumbs into separate small bowl. Dip meatballs into egg mixture then into bread crumbs. Arrange on ungreased baking sheet. Bake in 450°F (230°C) oven for 15 to 16 minutes, turning once or twice until crispy and golden. Drain. Makes about 8 dozen (96) meatballs.

6 meatballs: 286 Calories; 9.8 g Total Fat; 525 mg Sodium; 29 g Protein; 18 g Carbohydrate; trace Dietary Fiber

---

To Make Ahead And Freeze: Place baked meatballs in single layer on baking sheet. Freeze for 2 hours then remove to freezer bag. Label. Freeze for up to 3 months. To serve from frozen state, see Tip, page 30.

Select-A-Meal: See page 12.

Patties

(BASE RECIPE)

Use with any of the sauces that follow on pages 31 to 37.

Dry bread crumbs	½ cup	125 mL
Salt	1½ tsp.	7 mL
Pepper	½ tsp.	2 mL
Worcestershire sauce	2 tsp.	10 mL
Finely chopped onion	⅓ cup	75 mL
Water	½ cup	125 mL
Lean ground beef	2 lbs.	900 g

Stir first 6 ingredients together well in large bowl.

Add ground beef. Mix well. Shape beef mixture into 16 patties, using ¼ cup (60 mL) for each. Brown patties on both sides on medium-high in non-stick frying pan until fully cooked. Cool. Makes 16 patties.

1 patty: 116 Calories; 6.2 g Total Fat; 310 mg Sodium; 11 g Protein; 3 g Carbohydrate; trace Dietary Fiber

To Make Ahead And Freeze: Place browned patties in single layer on baking sheet. Freeze for 2 hours then place in freezer bag. Label. Freeze for up to 3 months. To serve from frozen state, see Tip, below.

Select-A-Meal: See page 12.

 Put desired number of thawed meatballs or patties and choice of sauce into an appropriate size casserole dish. As a general rule, use about 1 cup (250 mL) sauce to about 24 meatballs (4 servings). Cover. Bake in 325°F (160°C) oven for 30 to 40 minutes or heat in saucepan until hot. To serve from frozen state, empty sauce into medium saucepan. Heat on medium-low, stirring often. Add frozen meatballs or patties. Cover. Simmer for about 10 minutes until heated through. If necessary, add a bit of milk or water to thin to desired consistency.

Mushroom–Sauced Patties

The apple juice gives the sauce a wine-like flavor.
Try the Mushroom Sauce with Corn And Pepper Pancakes, page 57.

◆ **Base Recipe: (Choose one)**
   Patties, page 30; Meatballs, page 28;
      Breaded Meatballs, page 29

MUSHROOM SAUCE		
Margarine (or butter)	2 tbsp.	30 mL
Chopped fresh mushrooms	2 cups	500 mL
Chopped onion	1/3 cup	75 mL
All-purpose flour	1/4 cup	60 mL
Chicken bouillon powder	1 1/2 tsp.	7 mL
Worcestershire sauce	1/2 tsp.	2 mL
Salt	1/4 tsp.	1 mL
Pepper	1/8 tsp.	0.5 mL
Paprika	1/2 tsp.	2 mL
Milk	2 cups	500 mL
Apple juice	1/2 cup	125 mL

Base Recipe: Thaw Patties or Meatballs.

Mushroom Sauce: Melt margarine in frying pan. Add mushrooms and onion. Sauté until soft and liquid is evaporated. Remove from heat.

Mix in flour, bouillon powder, Worcestershire sauce, salt, pepper and paprika. Return to heat.

Stir in milk and apple juice. Simmer for about 4 minutes, stirring often, until mixture is boiling and thickened. Add patties. Simmer until heated through. Makes 2 3/4 cups (675 mL) sauce.

1/4 cup (60 mL) sauce only: 62 Calories; 2.8 g Total Fat; 202 mg Sodium; 2 g Protein; 7 g Carbohydrate; trace Dietary Fiber

Mushroom Sauce pictured on page 126.

To Make Ahead And Freeze: Double or triple Mushroom Sauce recipe. Divide among 3 cup (750 mL) freezer containers. Label. Freeze for up to 3 months. To serve with meatballs or patties from frozen state, see Tip, page 30.

Select-A-Meal: See page 12.

Stroganoff Meatballs

Mellow mushrooms in an excellent tangy, creamy sauce.

◆ **Base Recipe: (Choose one)**
   Meatballs, page 28; Breaded Meatballs,
      page 29; Patties, page 30

STROGANOFF SAUCE		
Margarine (or butter)	1 tbsp.	15 mL
Chopped onion	½ cup	125 mL
Chopped fresh mushrooms	1 cup	250 mL
All-purpose flour	2 tbsp.	30 mL
Water	¾ cup	175 mL
Beef bouillon powder	2 tsp.	10 mL
Salt	½ tsp.	2 mL
Pepper	⅛ tsp.	0.5 mL
Light sour cream	1 cup	250 mL
Paprika	¼ tsp.	1 mL

Base Recipe: Thaw Meatballs or Patties.

Stroganoff Sauce: Melt margarine in frying pan. Add onion and mushrooms. Sauté until soft and liquid is evaporated.

Mix in flour. Stir in water. Heat and stir on medium until boiling.

Add bouillon powder, salt, pepper, sour cream, paprika and meatballs. Heat and stir until heated through. Makes about 2 cups (500 mL) sauce.

¼ cup (60 mL) sauce only: 56 Calories; 3.8 g Total Fat; 349 mg Sodium; 2 g Protein; 4 g Carbohydrate; trace Dietary Fiber

To Make Ahead And Freeze: Double or triple Stroganoff Sauce recipe. Divide among 2 cup (500 mL) freezer containers. Label. Freeze for up to 3 months. To serve with meatballs or patties from frozen state, see Tip, page 30.

Select-A-Meal: See page 12.

Cranberry Chili Meatballs

Jewel-colored sauce. Bite from chili sauce complements
sweet cranberry flavor and savory meatballs.

♦ **Base Recipe: (Choose one)**
  Meatballs, page 28; Breaded Meatballs,
  page 29; Patties, page 30

CRANBERRY CHILI SAUCE

Ketchup	¹/₂ cup	125 mL
Chili sauce	¹/₂ cup	125 mL
Cranberry jelly	1 cup	250 mL
White vinegar	1 tsp.	5 mL

Base Recipe: Thaw Meatballs or Patties.

Cranberry Chili Sauce: Stir all 4 ingredients in medium saucepan. Add meatballs. Simmer until heated through. Makes 2 cups (500 mL) sauce.

¹/₄ cup (60 mL) sauce only: 146 Calories; 0.2 g Total Fat; 462 mg Sodium; 1 g Protein; 37 g Carbohydrate; 2 g Dietary Fiber

---

To Make Ahead And Freeze: Double or triple Cranberry Chili Sauce recipe. Divide among 2 cup (500 mL) freezer containers. Label. Freeze for up to 3 months. To serve with meatballs or patties from frozen state, see Tip, page 30.

Select-A-Meal: See page 12.

Paré Pointer

All kids know that the four seasons are
salt, pepper, ketchup, and mustard.

Dilly Meatballs

These are smothered in a perfect creamy sauce.

◆ **Base Recipe: (Choose one)**
   Meatballs, page 28; Breaded Meatballs,
     page 29; Patties, page 30

DILLY SAUCE

Water	1 cup	250 mL
All-purpose flour	2 tbsp.	30 mL
Light sour cream	1 cup	250 mL
Ketchup	1 tbsp.	15 mL
Dill weed	1 tbsp.	15 mL
Salt	½ tsp.	2 mL
Pepper	⅛ tsp.	0.5 mL

Base Recipe: Thaw Meatballs or Patties.

Dilly Sauce: Gradually stir water into flour in medium saucepan. Stir in sour cream, ketchup, dill weed, salt and pepper. Heat and stir until boiling and thickened. Add meatballs. Simmer until heated through. Makes 2¼ cups (560 mL) sauce.

¼ cup (60 mL) sauce only: 34 Calories; 1.9 g Total Fat; 186 mg Sodium; 1 g Protein; 3 g Carbohydrate; trace Dietary Fiber

Make Ahead And Freeze: Double or triple Dilly Sauce recipe. Divide among 2½ cup (625 mL) freezer containers. Label. Freeze for up to 3 months. To serve with meatballs or patties from frozen state, see Tip, page 30.

Select-A-Meal: See page 12.

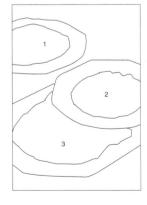

1. Thai Chicken And Noodles, page 46
2. Pineapple Chicken, page 47
3. Chicken Chop Suey, page 49

Props Courtesy Of: The Bay

Sweet And Sour Meatballs

This smooth sauce clings to the meatballs or patties, making them irresistible.

◆ **Base Recipe: (Choose one)**
  Meatballs, page 28; Breaded Meatballs,
    page 29; Patties, page 30

SWEET AND SOUR SAUCE		
Brown sugar, packed	1⅓ cups	325 mL
All-purpose flour	3 tbsp.	50 mL
Water	⅔ cup	150 mL
White vinegar	½ cup	125 mL
Ketchup	1 tbsp.	15 mL
Low-sodium soy sauce	1 tbsp.	15 mL

Base Recipe: Thaw Meatballs or Patties.

Sweet And Sour Sauce: Mix brown sugar and flour well in medium saucepan.

Stir in water, vinegar, ketchup and soy sauce. Heat and stir until boiling and thickened. Add meatballs. Simmer until heated through. Makes about 2 cups (500 mL) sauce.

¼ cup (60 mL) sauce only: 161 Calories; trace Total Fat; 116 mg Sodium; 1 g Protein; 41 g Carbohydrate; trace Dietary Fiber

---

To Make Ahead And Freeze: Double or triple Sweet And Sour Sauce recipe. Divide among 2 cup (500 mL) freezer containers. Label. Freeze for up to 3 months. To serve with meatballs or patties from frozen state, see Tip, page 30.

Select-A-Meal: See page 12.

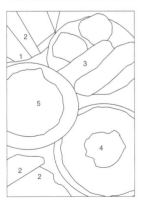

1. Marinated Beef Strips, page 38
2. Precut Veggies, page 39
3. Fast Fajitas, page 43
4. Teriyaki Stir-Fry, page 45
5. Quick Stroganoff, page 44

Props Courtesy Of: The Bay

Marinated Beef Strips

(BASE RECIPES)

Three pounds (1.4 kg) of steak are enough to make all four packages.

◆ **Package #1**
(use in Teriyaki Stir-Fry, page 45)

Sirloin or flank steak, trimmed (not previously frozen)	³/₄ lb.	340 g
Low-sodium soy sauce	1 tbsp.	15 mL
Garlic clove, minced	1	1
Ground ginger	¹/₂ tsp.	2 mL
Brown sugar, packed	¹/₂ tsp.	2 mL
Lemon juice	1¹/₂ tsp.	7 mL

Label sealable plastic freezer bag as #1, using permanent marker. Cut steak across grain into ¹/₈ inch (3 mm) strips. Place in bag.

Stir remaining 5 ingredients in cup. Pour into bag. Squeeze out air. Seal. Squeeze and press bag to distribute flavor ingredients. Makes 1 package.

1 package: 573 Calories; 25.2 g Total Fat; 839 mg Sodium; 76 g Protein; 6 g Carbohydrate; trace Dietary Fiber

◆ **Package #2**
(use in Fast Fajitas, page 43)

Sirloin or flank steak, trimmed (not previously frozen)	³/₄ lb.	340 g
Lime (or lemon) juice	2 tsp.	10 mL
Salsa	1 tbsp.	15 mL
Dried crushed chilies	¹/₄ tsp.	1 mL
Ground cumin	¹/₄ tsp.	1 mL

Follow method as in Package #1 but label #2. Makes 1 package.

1 package: 560 Calories; 25.4 g Total Fat; 453 mg Sodium; 75 g Protein; 4 g Carbohydrate; trace Dietary Fiber

◆ **Package #3**
(use in Quick Stroganoff, page 44)

Sirloin or flank steak, trimmed (not previously frozen)	³/₄ lb.	340 g
Garlic clove, minced	1	1

Follow method as in Package #1 but label #3. Makes 1 package.

1 package: 549 Calories; 25.2 g Total Fat; 212 mg Sodium; 75 g Protein; 1 g Carbohydrate; trace Dietary Fiber

◆ **Package #4**
(use in Thai Beef And Noodles, page 47)

Sirloin or flank steak, trimmed (not previously frozen)	¾ lb.	340 g
Brown sugar, packed	1 tsp.	5 mL
Lime (or lemon) juice	2 tsp.	10 mL
Dried crushed chilies	¼ tsp.	1 mL
Finely grated gingerroot	1 tbsp.	15 mL
Sesame oil	½ tsp.	2 mL

Follow method as in Package #1 but label #4. Makes 1 package.

1 package: 591 Calories; 27.2 g Total Fat; 221 mg Sodium; 75 g Protein; 8 g Carbohydrate; trace Dietary Fiber

Pictured on page 36.

Make Ahead And Freeze: Packages #1, #2, #3 and #4 can be frozen for up to 4 months.

Precut Veggies

(BASE RECIPE)

Use in any recipe requiring chopped fresh vegetables. Great to have ready for making Fast Fajitas, page 43; Quick Stroganoff, page 44; Teriyaki Stir-Fry, page 45; and Broccoli Pasta Bake, page 48.

Large broccoli crown	1	1
Medium carrots	5	5
Whole fresh mushrooms	3 cups	750 mL
Medium regular (or red) onions	4	4
Medium green peppers	2	2
Medium red peppers	3	3
Medium yellow peppers	2	2

Cut broccoli into 1 inch (2.5 cm) florets. Finely slice stalk. Thinly slice carrots on diagonal or julienne. Clean mushrooms with dry towel or mushroom brush. Thinly slice. Peel and cut onions in half lengthwise. Cut lengthwise into ½ inch (12 mm) slices. Separate layers. Seed, and cut all peppers into 2 x ½ inch (5 x 1.2 cm) slices or strips. Put each vegetable into separate sealable storage bag, squeezing out air. Seal.

Pictured on page 36.

Make Ahead And Store: Keep in airtight bags in refrigerator for up to 10 days. Do not freeze.

Marinated Chicken Strips

(BASE RECIPE)

Three pounds (1.4 kg) of chicken are enough to make all four packages.

◆ **Package #1**
(use in Teriyaki Stir-Fry, page 45;
Pineapple Chicken, page 47; or
Chicken Chop Suey, page 49)

Boneless, skinless chicken breast halves (about 3), not previously frozen	³/₄ lb.	340 g
Low-sodium soy sauce	1 tbsp.	15 mL
Garlic clove, minced	1	1
Ground ginger	¹/₂ tsp.	2 mL
Brown sugar, packed	¹/₂ tsp.	2 mL
Lime (or lemon) juice	1¹/₂ tsp.	7 mL

Label sealable plastic freezer bag as #1, using permanent marker. Cut chicken across the grain into ¹/₈ inch (3 mm) strips. Place in bag.

Stir remaining 5 ingredients in cup. Pour into bag. Squeeze out air. Seal. Squeeze and press bag to distribute flavor ingredients. Makes 1 package.

1 package: 402 Calories; 4.3 g Total Fat; 849 mg Sodium; 80 g Protein; 6 g Carbohydrate; trace Dietary Fiber

◆ **Package #2**
(use in Fast Fajitas, page 43)

Boneless, skinless chicken breast halves (about 3), not previously frozen	³/₄ lb.	340 g
Lime (or lemon) juice	2 tsp.	10 mL
Salsa	1 tbsp.	15 mL
Dried crushed chilies	¹/₄ tsp.	1 mL
Ground cumin	¹/₄ tsp.	1 mL

Follow method as in Package #1 but label #2. Makes 1 package.

1 package: 389 Calories; 4.5 g Total Fat; 462 mg Sodium; 79 g Protein; 4 g Carbohydrate; trace Dietary Fiber

◆ **Package #3**
(use in Quick Stroganoff, page 44, or
Broccoli Pasta Bake, page 48)

Boneless, skinless chicken breast halves (about 3), not previously frozen	¾ **lb.**	**340 g**
Garlic clove, minced	**1**	**1**

Follow method as in Package #1 but label #3. Makes 1 package.

1 package: 378 Calories; 4.2 g Total Fat; 222 mg Sodium; 79 g Protein; 1 g Carbohydrate; trace Dietary Fiber

◆ **Package #4 CHICKEN STRIPS**
(use in Thai Chicken And Noodles,
page 46)

Boneless, skinless chicken breast halves (about 3), not previously frozen	¾ **lb.**	**340 g**
Brown sugar, packed	1 tsp.	5 mL
Lime (or lemon) juice	2 tsp.	10 mL
Dried crushed chilies	¼ tsp.	1 mL
Finely grated gingerroot	1 tbsp.	15 mL
Sesame oil	½ tsp.	2 mL

Follow method as in Package #1 but label #4. Makes 1 package.

1 package: 420 Calories; 6.2 g Total Fat; 230 mg Sodium; 79 g Protein; 8 g Carbohydrate; trace Dietary Fiber

---

To Make Ahead And Freeze: Packages #1, #2, #3 and #4 can be frozen for up to 4 months.

Paré Pointer

*One thing for sure is when frogs and rabbits make
beer, they start with hops.*

Mango Starter

(BASE RECIPE)

*Take advantage of mangoes when in season. This starter
is versatile for use in main dishes and as a dessert topping for ice cream
or cake. Use in Marengo Mango Chicken, page 50; Curried
Chicken, page 51; or Sweet And Sour Pork, page 52.*

Large fresh mangoes, firm but not hard (about 3½ lbs., 1.6 kg)	6	6
Water	1½ cups	375 mL
Brown sugar, packed	1 cup	250 mL

Peel off skin using a potato peeler or paring knife. Slice half mango off
both sides around pit. Section off slices around pit until pit is bare of flesh.
Cut larger pieces. Place mango pieces in large saucepan. Stir in water. Heat
on medium, stirring frequently, until boiling. Reduce heat. Cover. Simmer
for 3 to 4 minutes until mango is softened but not mushy. Stir in brown
sugar. Simmer for 5 minutes. Makes about 8¼ cups (2 L) or 1½ cups
(375 mL) per portion.

*1 portion: 335 Calories; 0.7 g Total Fat; 19 mg Sodium; 1 g Protein; 87 g Carbohydrate;
5 g Dietary Fiber*

Pictured on page 53.

To Make Ahead And Freeze: Divide among 5 sealable plastic freezer bags or
freezer containers. Label. Freeze for up to 2 months.

 *To quickly warm flour tortillas, sprinkle each tortilla with a few drops
of water. Wrap together in damp paper towel or tea towel. Microwave
for 1 to 2 minutes on medium power (50%). Or seal damp tortillas
in foil and heat in 325°F (160°C) oven for about 10 minutes. Keep
covered until your guests are ready for their second helping.*

Fast Fajitas

Not too spicy with plenty of flavorful vegetables. Serve with bowls of Cheddar cheese, sour cream, lettuce and diced tomatoes.

◆ **Base Recipe:**		
Marinated Beef Strips, page 38, Package #2 (see Note)	1	1
Cooking oil	2 tsp.	10 mL
Cooking oil	2 tsp.	10 mL
Precut Veggies, page 39		
Red onion	1½ cups	375 mL
Green pepper	1 cup	250 mL
Red pepper	1 cup	250 mL
Yellow pepper	1 cup	250 mL
Mushrooms	1 cup	250 mL
Freshly squeezed lime (or lemon) juice	1 tbsp.	15 mL
Ground cumin	⅛ tsp.	0.5 mL
Salt	½ tsp.	2 mL
Pepper	⅛ tsp.	0.5 mL
Salsa	¼ cup	60 mL
Large flour tortillas	6	6

Base Recipe: Thaw package of Beef Strips.

Stir-fry beef strips in first amount of hot cooking oil in frying pan or wok for 2 minutes or until cooked. Remove to bowl.

Heat second amount of cooking oil in frying pan. Add red onion, peppers and mushrooms. Stir. Cover. Heat on medium-high for 2 minutes.

Add next 4 ingredients. Stir, scraping up any browned bits in pan. Add reserved beef and any accumulated juices. Stir. Increase heat to high. Stir. Heat, uncovered, until moisture evaporates and mixture sizzles.

Stir in salsa. Remove from heat. Keep warm. Makes 4 cups (1 L) filling.

Fill warm tortillas (see Tip, page 42) with ½ to ¾ cup (125 to 175 mL) filling. Fold, envelope-style, to eat. Makes 6 fajitas.

1 fajita: 326 Calories; 8.3 g Total Fat; 673 mg Sodium; 20 g Protein; 43 g Carbohydrate; 3 g Dietary Fiber

Pictured on page 36.

Note: Substitute Marinated Beef Strips with Marinated Chicken Strips, page 40, if desired.

Quick Stroganoff

This meal can be on the table in the time it takes to cook the noodles.

◆ **Base Recipe:**

Marinated Beef Strips, page 38, Package #3	1	1
Cooking oil	1 tbsp.	15 mL
Precut Veggies, page 39		
Onion, chopped smaller	1/2 cup	125 mL
Mushrooms	2 cups	500 mL
Water	1 cup	250 mL
Beef bouillon powder	1 tbsp.	15 mL
Worcestershire sauce	1-2 tsp.	5-10 mL
Pepper	1/2 tsp.	2 mL
Ketchup	2 tbsp.	30 mL
Can of skim evaporated milk	13 1/2 oz.	385 mL
All-purpose flour	1/4 cup	60 mL
Light sour cream	1/2 cup	125 mL

Base Recipe: Thaw package of Beef Strips.

Stir-fry beef strips in hot cooking oil in large frying pan or wok for 1 minute. Add onion and mushrooms. Stir-fry for 5 minutes until onion is soft and mushrooms are brown. Add water, bouillon powder, Worcestershire sauce, pepper and ketchup. Bring to a boil.

Gradually whisk evaporated milk into flour in small bowl until smooth. Slowly stir into beef mixture. Boil for 1 minute.

Add sour cream just before serving. Heat through without boiling. Makes 4 cups (1 L). Serves 4.

1 serving: 340 Calories; 12.6 g Total Fat; 752 mg Sodium; 30 g Protein; 27 g Carbohydrate; 1 g Dietary Fiber

Pictured on page 36.

QUICK CHICKEN STROGANOFF: Use Package of #3 Chicken Strips, page 41, instead of beef strips. Substitute chicken bouillon powder for beef bouillon powder. Add a little gravy browner for color.

Progressive Recipes

Teriyaki Stir-Fry

A quick and easy supper. Serve over rice or rice noodles.

◆ Base Recipe:		
Marinated Beef Strips, page 38, Package #1 (see Note)	1	1
Water	½ cup	125 mL
Liquid beef (or chicken) bouillon (or powder)	½ tsp.	2 mL
Cornstarch	2 tsp.	10 mL
Hoisin sauce	1 tbsp.	15 mL
Granulated sugar	1 tsp.	5 mL
Low-sodium soy sauce	2 tsp.	10 mL
Cooking oil	2 tsp.	10 mL
Cooking oil	2 tsp.	10 mL
Precut Veggies, page 39		
Carrot	½ cup	125 mL
Onion	½ cup	125 mL
Green pepper	½ cup	125 mL
Red pepper	½ cup	125 mL
Yellow pepper	½ cup	125 mL
Mushrooms	½ cup	125 mL
Broccoli	1½ cups	375 mL
Can of sliced water chestnuts, drained	8 oz.	227 mL

Base Recipe: Thaw package of Beef Strips.

Combine first 6 ingredients in small cup. Set aside.

Stir-fry beef strips in first amount of hot cooking oil in frying pan or wok for 2 to 3 minutes until cooked. Remove to small bowl.

Heat second amount of cooking oil in frying pan. Stir-fry carrot and onion for 1 minute. Add peppers, mushrooms, broccoli and water chestnuts. Stir-fry for 3 to 4 minutes until peppers and broccoli are tender-crisp. Add beef strips. Stir cornstarch mixture. Add to beef mixture. Stir continually until boiling and thickened. Makes 6 cups (1.5 L). Serves 4.

1 serving: 270 Calories; 11.3 g Total Fat; 589 mg Sodium; 22 g Protein; 21 g Carbohydrate; 3 g Dietary Fiber

Pictured on page 36.

Note: Substitute Marinated Beef Strips with Marinated Chicken Strips, page 40, if desired.

Thai Chicken And Noodles

Ginger and a hint of hot chilies, topped with crunchy peanuts make this dish deliciously different.

◆ **Base Recipe:**		
Marinated Chicken Strips, page 41, Package #4	1	1
Chili sauce	¼ cup	60 mL
Fancy (mild) molasses	2 tbsp.	30 mL
Water	2 tbsp.	30 mL
Low-sodium soy sauce	2 tbsp.	30 mL
Rice (or apple cider) vinegar	2 tbsp.	30 mL
Brown sugar, packed	1 tsp.	5 mL
Cornstarch	2 tsp.	10 mL
Cooking oil	2 tsp.	10 mL
Precut Veggies, page 39		
Carrot	¾ cup	175 mL
Onion	¾ cup	175 mL
Red and yellow pepper strips	2 cups	500 mL
Chopped green onion	¼ cup	60 mL
Fresh bean sprouts	2 cups	500 mL
Boiling water, to cover		
Rice vermicelli	8 oz.	225 g
Chopped salted peanuts	¼ cup	60 mL
Sesame seeds, toasted	2 tsp.	10 mL

Base Recipe: Thaw package of Chicken Strips.

Combine first 7 ingredients in small cup. Set sauce aside.

Add cooking oil to frying pan or wok. Heat on medium-high. Add chicken strips. Stir-fry for 1 minute. Add carrot and onion. Stir-fry for 2 minutes. Add pepper strips, green onion and bean sprouts. Stir-fry for 1 to 2 minutes until chicken is cooked and vegetables are softened. Stir cornstarch mixture. Add to chicken mixture. Stir continually until boiling and thickened. Makes 4 cups (1 L).

Pour boiling water over rice vermicelli to cover in large bowl. Let stand for 5 minutes. Drain. Rinse with warm water. Drain well. Arrange on platter. Top with chicken mixture.

Sprinkle with peanuts and sesame seeds. Serves 4.

(continued on next page)

1 serving: 521 Calories; 9.2 g Total Fat; 692 mg Sodium; 30 g Protein; 81 g Carbohydrate; 6 g Dietary Fiber

Pictured on page 35.

THAI BEEF AND NOODLES: Use 1 package of #4 Beef Strips, page 39, instead of chicken strips.

Pineapple Chicken

Have a bowl of hot rice ready before you start as this delicious meal takes only minutes to prepare.

◆ Base Recipe:		
Marinated Chicken Strips, page 40, Package #1	1	1
Finely chopped onion	²/₃ cup	150 mL
Cooking oil	2 tsp.	10 mL
All-purpose flour	1 tbsp.	15 mL
Precut Veggies, page 39		
Green pepper	²/₃ cup	150 mL
Red pepper	²/₃ cup	150 mL
Can of pineapple tidbits, with juice	14 oz.	398 mL
Brown sugar, packed	2 tbsp.	30 mL
Barbecue sauce	2 tbsp.	30 mL
Lemon juice	2 tsp.	10 mL
Salt	¹/₂ tsp.	2 mL
Pepper	¹/₄ tsp.	1 mL

Base Recipe: Thaw package of Chicken Strips.

Sauté chicken strips and onion in cooking oil in frying pan for 4 minutes until chicken is opaque. Sprinkle with flour. Stir. Toss to coat.

Add remaining 8 ingredients. Stir. Cover. Cook on medium for 10 to 12 minutes until bubbling and peppers are tender-crisp. Makes 4 cups (1 L).

1 cup (250 mL): 246 Calories; 3.8 g Total Fat; 621 mg Sodium; 22 g Protein; 32 g Carbohydrate; 3 g Dietary Fiber

Pictured on page 35.

Broccoli Pasta Bake

Comfort food!

◆ **Base Recipe:**		
Marinated Chicken Strips, page 41, Package #3	1	1
Rotini pasta (about 6 oz., 170 g)	2¼ cups	560 mL
Boiling water	3 qts.	3 L
Salt	1 tbsp.	15 mL
Chopped broccoli	3 cups	750 mL
Margarine (or butter)	1 tbsp.	15 mL
Precut Veggies, page 39		
Onion	½ cup	125 mL
Mushrooms	1 cup	250 mL
Grated carrot, packed	⅓ cup	75 mL
Water	1½ cups	375 mL
Chicken bouillon powder	2 tsp.	10 mL
Parsley flakes	2 tsp.	10 mL
Can of skim evaporated milk	13½ oz.	385 mL
All-purpose flour	¼ cup	60 mL
Low-fat salad dressing	2 tbsp.	30 mL
Grated light sharp Cheddar cheese	⅔ cup	150 mL
Fresh bread crumbs (1 slice, processed)	½ cup	125 mL

Base Recipe: Thaw package of Chicken Strips.

Cook pasta in boiling water and salt in large uncovered pot or Dutch oven for 8 minutes. Add broccoli. Cook for 3 minutes until pasta is tender but firm. Drain. Rinse well with cold water. Drain. Return to pot.

Melt margarine in frying pan. Add onion. Sauté for 3 minutes until softened. Add mushrooms and carrot. Add chicken strips. Sauté for about 8 minutes until liquid is evaporated and chicken is cooked.

Add water, bouillon powder and parsley flakes. Stir. Bring to a boil.

Gradually stir evaporated milk into flour in small bowl until smooth. Add dressing. Mix. Add to chicken mixture. Heat and stir until boiling and thickened. Pour over pasta mixture. Stir. Pour into greased 3 quart (3 L) casserole.

(continued on next page)

Combine cheese and bread crumbs in small bowl. Sprinkle over casserole. Bake, uncovered, in a 325°F (160°C) oven for 30 minutes. Serves 4.

1 serving: 532 Calories; 11.7 g Total Fat; 783 mg Sodium; 43 g Protein; 63 g Carbohydrate; 4 g Dietary Fiber

To Make Ahead: Assemble early in day or night before. Cover. Chill. To serve, bake as above. Do not freeze.

Chicken Chop Suey

While the rice cooks, stir-fry the rest and dinner's ready in 30 minutes.

◆ Base Recipe: Marinated Chicken Strips, page 40, Package #1	1	1
Low-sodium soy sauce	2 tbsp.	30 mL
Cornstarch	1 tbsp.	15 mL
Water	1/3 cup	75 mL
Liquid chicken bouillon (or powder)	1/2 tsp.	2 mL
Cooking oil	4 tsp.	20 mL
Precut Veggies, page 39		
Onion	2/3 cup	150 mL
Mushrooms	1 cup	250 mL
Green pepper	2/3 cup	150 mL
Celery, thinly sliced on diagonal	1 cup	250 mL
Fresh bean sprouts (about 12 oz., 340 g)	2 cups	500 mL

Base Recipe: Thaw package of Chicken Strips.

Combine first 4 ingredients in small cup. Stir well. Set aside.

Stir-fry chicken strips in hot cooking oil in frying pan for about 3 minutes until no longer pink. Remove with slotted spoon to small bowl.

Stir-fry onion, mushrooms, green pepper and celery for 4 minutes until tender-crisp. Add chicken. Stir cornstarch mixture. Stir slowly into chicken mixture until boiling and thickened.

Add bean sprouts. Toss. Cover. Cook for 2 minutes. Stir. Makes 5 cups (1.25 L). Serves 4.

1 serving: 207 Calories; 6.1 g Total Fat; 642 mg Sodium; 25 g Protein; 15 g Carbohydrate; 3 g Dietary Fiber

Pictured on page 35.

Marengo Mango Chicken

Delicate hint of white wine and thyme. Serve over rice or pasta.

◆ Base Recipe: package of Mango Starter, page 42	1	1
Chicken parts, bone in, skin removed	4 lbs.	1.8 kg
Cooking oil	1 tbsp.	15 mL
Chopped onion	1 cup	250 mL
Sliced fresh mushrooms	2 cups	500 mL
Garlic powder (or 2 cloves, minced)	½ tsp.	2 mL
Pepper	½ tsp.	2 mL
Cayenne pepper	⅛ tsp.	0.5 mL
Can of stewed tomatoes, with juice, chopped	28 oz.	796 mL
Dry (or alcohol-free) white wine	½ cup	125 mL
Bay leaves	2	2
Chopped fresh parsley	2 tsp.	10 mL
Dried thyme	1 tsp.	5 mL
Ground rosemary	¼ tsp.	1 mL
Seasoned salt	1 tsp.	5 mL
Cornstarch	6 tbsp.	100 mL

Base Recipe: Thaw package of Mango Starter.

Arrange chicken in medium roaster, ungreased 4 quart (4 L) casserole or two 2 quart (2 L) casseroles.

Heat cooking oil in large frying pan. Add onion, mushrooms and garlic powder. Sauté, stirring frequently, until softened. Sprinkle with pepper and cayenne pepper. Stir. Spoon over chicken.

Put next 7 ingredients into same frying pan. Stir. Heat until boiling. Pour over chicken mixture. Cover. Bake in 350°F (175°C) oven for 1 hour.

Remove ½ cup (125 mL) juice from Mango Starter. Stir into cornstarch in small dish. Stir remaining Mango Starter into chicken mixture. Stir cornstarch mixture. Add to hot chicken mixture. Stir well. Bake, uncovered, for 20 minutes until sauce is thickened. Discard bay leaves. Serves 8.

(continued on next page)

1 serving: 240 Calories; 5.2 g Total Fat; 365 mg Sodium; 25 g Protein; 24 g Carbohydrate; 2 g Dietary Fiber

Pictured on page 53.

To Make Ahead: Assemble early in day or night before. Cover. Chill. To serve, bake as above, adding Mango Starter and juice to thicken. Do not freeze.

Curried Chicken

*The aroma of this cooking will make
you hungry! Serve over couscous or rice.*

◆ Base Recipe: package of Mango Starter, page 42	1	1
Boneless, skinless chicken breast halves (about 4), cut bite size	1 lb.	454 g
Cooking oil	2 tsp.	10 mL
Salt	1/2 tsp.	2 mL
Dried crushed chilies	1/4 tsp.	1 mL
Medium onion, cut lengthwise into wedges	1	1
Garlic cloves, minced	2	2
Coarsely grated carrot	1/2 cup	125 mL
Water	1/4 cup	60 mL
Raisins	1/2 cup	125 mL
Curry powder	1/2 tsp.	2 mL
Frozen peas	2/3 cup	150 mL
Mango (or apple) juice	1 cup	250 mL
Cornstarch	2 tsp.	10 mL

Base Recipe: Thaw package of Mango Starter.

Sauté chicken in cooking oil in frying pan for 2 minutes until just opaque. Sprinkle with salt and chilies. Add onion, garlic and carrot. Sauté for about 5 minutes, stirring frequently, until bottom of pan is starting to brown.

Stir in Mango Starter, water, raisins and curry powder. Cover. Simmer for 10 minutes, stirring occasionally.

Stir in frozen peas.

Stir mango juice into cornstarch in small dish. Stir into chicken mixture. Heat and stir until bubbling and thickened. Serves 4.

1 serving: 363 Calories; 4.3 g Total Fat; 459 mg Sodium; 29 g Protein; 54 g Carbohydrate; 4 g Dietary Fiber

Pictured on page 53.

Sweet And Sour Pork

Made with a thick and flavorful sauce.
Serve over rice or couscous.

♦ **Base Recipe: package of** Mango Starter, page 42	1	1
Pork loin, trimmed and cut into ¾ inch (2 cm) cubes	1 lb.	454 g
Cooking oil	2 tsp.	10 mL
Diced red onion	⅔ cup	150 mL
Diced green, red or yellow pepper	⅔ cup	150 mL
Garlic clove, minced (optional)	1	1
White vinegar	¼ cup	60 mL
Chili sauce	¼ cup	60 mL

Base Recipe: Thaw package of Mango Starter.

Sauté pork in cooking oil in frying pan until starting to brown.

Add onion, diced pepper and garlic. Sauté until vegetables are soft and pork is browned.

Stir in vinegar, chili sauce and Mango Starter. Cover. Simmer for 30 minutes, stirring occasionally, until pork is tender. Serves 4.

1 serving: 268 Calories; 5.4 g Total Fat; 305 mg Sodium; 25 g Protein; 31 g Carbohydrate; 3 g Dietary Fiber

Pictured on page 53.

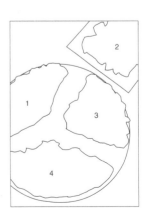

1. Curried Chicken, page 51
2. Mango Starter, page 42
3. Sweet And Sour Pork, above
4. Marengo Mango Chicken, page 50

Props Courtesy Of: Chintz & Company
                     The Bay

Corn Bread Mix

(BASE RECIPE)

Use in Cheese And Onion Muffins, page 56, or
Corn And Pepper Pancakes, page 57.

Yellow cornmeal	5 cups	1.25 L
All-purpose flour	5 cups	1.25 L
Skim milk powder	2 cups	500 mL
Granulated sugar	1 cup	250 mL
Brown sugar, packed	½ cup	125 mL
Baking powder	6 tbsp.	100 mL
Salt	1 tbsp.	15 mL
Cooking oil	1 cup	250 mL

Stir first 7 ingredients in large bowl.

Mix in cooking oil until mixture is crumbly. Makes 15 cups (3.74 L).

1 cup (250 mL): 611 Calories; 16.7 g Total Fat; 579 mg Sodium; 15 g Protein; 100 g Carbohydrate; 4 g Dietary Fiber

Pictured on page 54.

Make Ahead And Store: Empty into airtight container. Label. Store in cupboard for up to 6 weeks, or up to 2 months in refrigerator.

1. Corn Bread Mix, above
2. Corn And Pepper Pancakes, page 57
3. Jamtart Muffins, page 56
4. Cheese And Onion Muffins, page 56

Props Courtesy Of: Chintz & Company
                     The Bay
                     X/S Wares

Cheese And Onion Muffins

Serve these warm with soup or salad.

♦ Base Recipe: Corn Bread Mix, page 55	2 cups	500 mL
Green onion, finely sliced	1	1
Grated light sharp Cheddar cheese	²/₃ cup	150 mL
Cayenne pepper	¹/₈ tsp.	0.5 mL
Water	²/₃ cup	150 mL
Large egg, fork-beaten	1	1

Base Recipe: Stir Corn Bread Mix before measuring into medium bowl.

Add next 3 ingredients. Make a well in center.

Pour water and beaten egg into well. Stir just to combine. Don't overmix. Spoon batter into 12 greased muffin cups. Bake in 400°F (205°C) oven for 12 minutes. Makes 12 muffins.

1 muffin: 128 Calories; 4.5 g Total Fat; 143 mg Sodium; 5 g Protein; 17 g Carbohydrate; 1 g Dietary Fiber

Pictured on page 54.

To Make Ahead: Bake up to 2 days ahead.

To Freeze: Bake, cool and wrap. Label. Freeze for up to 3 months. To serve, see Tip, page 61.

Jamtart Muffins

There's jam in every bite!

♦ Base Recipe: Corn Bread Mix, page 55	2¹/₂ cups	625 mL
Light sour cream	³/₄ cup	175 mL
Water	¹/₃ cup	75 mL
Large egg, fork-beaten	1	1
Raspberry jam	¹/₄ cup	60 mL

Base Recipe: Stir Corn Bread Mix before measuring into medium bowl.

Combine next 3 ingredients in small bowl. Stir into corn bread mix until just moistened. Spoon batter into 12 greased muffin cups.

(continued on next page)

Poke 1 tsp. (5 mL) jam into center of each muffin. Bake at 375°F (190°C) for 12 minutes. Makes 12 muffins.

1 muffin: 166 Calories; 5 g Total Fat; 135 mg Sodium; 4 g Protein; 26 g Carbohydrate; 1 g Dietary Fiber

Pictured on page 54.

To Make Ahead: Bake up to 2 days ahead. Cover.

To Freeze: Bake, cool and wrap. Label. Freeze for up to 3 months. To serve, see Tip, page 61.

Corn And Pepper Pancakes

Pancakes with a delicious crunch. Try these with Mushroom Sauce, page 31, or your favorite pancake syrup.

◆ Base Recipe: Corn Bread Mix, page 55	2 cups	500 mL
Frozen corn, cooked, drained and cooled	⅓ cup	75 mL
Finely chopped red pepper	¼ cup	60 mL
Finely sliced green onion	2 tbsp.	30 mL
Large eggs, fork-beaten	2	2
Water	¾ cup	175 mL
Cooking oil	1 tbsp.	15 mL

Base Recipe: Stir Corn Bread Mix before measuring into medium bowl.

Add corn, red pepper and green onion. Stir. Make a well in center.

Pour beaten eggs and water into well. Stir just to combine.

Brush non-stick frying pan with about 1 tbsp. (15 mL) cooking oil. Drop batter by ¼ cup (60 mL) onto hot surface. Cook for 1 to 2 minutes. Turn over. Cook for 1 minute until golden. Lightly stir batter occasionally to redistribute vegetables. Brush surface with more cooking oil as needed. Serve hot. Makes 10 pancakes.

1 pancake: 155 Calories; 5.7 g Total Fat; 127 mg Sodium; 4 g Protein; 22 g Carbohydrate; 1 g Dietary Fiber

Pictured on page 54.

To Make Ahead And Freeze: Bake, cool and wrap. Label. Freeze for up to 3 months. To serve, see Tip, page 61.

Surprise Corn Bread

The surprise is the combined flavors of cheese and broccoli.

◆ Base Recipe: Corn Bread Mix, page 55	2 cups	500 mL
Large eggs	3	3
Light sour cream	½ cup	125 mL
Water	¼ cup	60 mL
Grated light sharp Cheddar cheese	1 cup	250 mL
Frozen chopped broccoli, thawed, patted dry with paper towel and chopped further into ½ inch (12 mm) pieces	2 cups	500 mL

Base Recipe: Stir Corn Bread Mix before measuring into small bowl.

Beat eggs in large bowl. Add sour cream and water. Mix. Stir in Corn Bread Mix until just combined. Add cheese and broccoli. Mix gently. Turn into greased 8 x 8 inch (20 x 20 cm) pan. Bake in 375°F (190°C) oven for 30 to 35 minutes until browned. A wooden pick inserted in center should come out clean. Cuts into 12 pieces.

1 piece: 169 Calories; 6.8 g Total Fat; 185 mg Sodium; 8 g Protein; 19 g Carbohydrate; 2 g Dietary Fiber

Pictured on front cover.

To Make Ahead: Bake. Cool and cover up to 1 to 2 days ahead. Heat, covered, in 325°F (160°C) oven for about 20 minutes until warm.

To Freeze: Bake, cool and wrap. Label. Freeze for up to 3 months. To serve, see Tip, page 61.

Whole Wheat Biscuit Mix

(BASE RECIPE)

Use in Seed And Cheese Wedges, page 59, or Mini Cheese Loaves, page 60.

All-purpose flour	3 cups	750 mL
Whole wheat flour	3 cups	750 mL
Baking powder	4½ tbsp.	67 mL
Brown sugar, packed	1 tbsp.	15 mL
Salt	1½ tsp.	7 mL
Cooking oil	1 cup	250 mL

(continued on next page)

Combine first 5 ingredients in large bowl.

Stir in cooking oil until mixture is crumbly. Makes about 8 cups (2 L).

1 cup (250 mL): 613 Calories; 30.2 g Total Fat; 541 mg Sodium; 12 g Protein; 77 g Carbohydrate; 8 g Dietary Fiber

---

Make Ahead And Store: Empty into airtight container. Label. Store in cupboard for up to 4 weeks.

Seed And Cheese Wedges

Delicious hot from the oven and spread with butter.

◆ **Base Recipe: Whole Wheat Biscuit Mix, page 58**	2½ cups	625 mL
Grated light sharp Cheddar cheese	⅔ cup	150 mL
Roasted salted sunflower seeds	2 tbsp.	30 mL
Finely chopped green onion	2 tbsp.	30 mL
Garlic powder	⅛ tsp.	0.5 mL
Milk	¾ cup	175 mL

Base Recipe: Spoon Whole Wheat Biscuit Mix into measuring cup and level off without packing. Empty into medium bowl.

Add cheese, sunflower seeds, green onion and garlic powder.

Stir in milk until moistened. Turn out onto lightly floured surface. Knead lightly 8 times. Pat dough into circle about 9 inches (22 cm) in diameter. Cut into 10 wedges. Place individual wedges on lightly greased baking sheet. Bake at 400°F (205°C) for 15 to 18 minutes until risen and browned. Makes 10 wedges.

1 wedge: 196 Calories; 10.1 g Total Fat; 209 mg Sodium; 6 g Protein; 21 g Carbohydrate; 2 g Dietary Fiber

Pictured on page 72.

To Make Ahead: Bake, cool and cover up to 1 day ahead.

To Freeze: Bake, cool and wrap. Label. Freeze for up to 3 months. To serve, see Tip, page 61.

Mini Cheese Loaves

*If you don't have the mini loaf pans, don't worry—these
taste just as delicious made into biscuits.*

◆ Base Recipe: Whole Wheat Biscuit Mix, page 58	2 cups	500 mL
Dill weed	1 tsp.	5 mL
Onion powder	1/4 tsp.	1 mL
Grated Parmesan cheese	2 tbsp.	30 mL
Bacon slices, cooked crisp and crumbled (or 2 tbsp., 30 mL, imitation bacon bits), see Tip, below	4	4
Large egg	1	1
Light creamed cottage cheese	1/2 cup	125 mL
Milk	1/4 cup	60 mL

Base Recipe: Spoon Whole Wheat Biscuit Mix into measuring cup and level off without packing. Empty into medium bowl.

Add next 4 ingredients. Make a well in center.

Process remaining 3 ingredients in blender until cottage cheese is almost smooth. Pour into well. Stir just to moisten. Knead dough 8 times on lightly floured surface. Lightly grease six 4 x 2 1/4 x 1 1/4 inch (10 x 5.75 x 3.5 cm) loaf pans. If pans are not available, pat into 6 x 8 inch (15 x 20 cm) rectangle and cut into 6 loaves. Place on greased baking sheet. Bake in 375°F (190°C) oven on center rack for about 20 minutes until golden. Makes 6.

1 mini loaf: 273 Calories; 13.7 g Total Fat; 335 mg Sodium; 11 g Protein; 27 g Carbohydrate; 3 g Dietary Fiber

---

To Make Ahead: Bake early in day or night before.

To Freeze: Bake, cool and wrap. Label. Freeze for up to 3 months. To serve, see Tip, page 61.

Make-Ahead Bacon Bits: Separate 1 lb. (454 g) bacon slices. Lay close together on large baking sheet with sides. Bake in 350°F (175°C) oven on bottom rack for about 10 minutes. Reverse sheets on racks. Bake for about 10 minutes until fat part of bacon is golden. The deeper golden, the crispier the bacon. Drain. Remove bacon to paper towels. Cool. Freeze in plastic bag or container. Label.

Cake Mix

(BASE RECIPE)

Use to make Apple Coffee Cake, page 62, or Gingerbread Cake, page 63.

Hard margarine (or butter), softened	1 cup	250 mL
Granulated sugar	2 cups	500 mL
Brown sugar, packed	2 cups	500 mL
Large eggs	4	4
All-purpose flour	6 cups	1.5 L
Baking powder	¼ cup	60 mL
Salt	2 tsp.	10 mL

Beat margarine for about 5 minutes until light-colored and increased in volume. Slowly add both sugars, about 2 tbsp. (30 mL) at a time. Beat until all sugar is added and mixture is light and fluffy. Beat in eggs, 1 at a time.

Combine remaining 3 dry ingredients in medium bowl. Gradually add to margarine mixture, beating on low until well mixed. Mixture will be crumbly but moist. Makes 4 packages.

1 package: 2090 Calories; 55.9 g Total Fat; 2085 mg Sodium; 27 g Protein; 374 g Carbohydrate; 7 g Dietary Fiber

Make Ahead And Store: Divide among 4 sealable plastic freezer bags or freezer containers, about 3¼ cups (800 mL) each. Label. Freeze for up to 6 weeks.

 tip

To serve muffins, pancakes, individual slices of loaves and pieces of cakes from frozen state, wrap loosely in foil. Heat in 350°F (175°C) oven for about 15 minutes. Whole loaves and cakes may require up to 30 minutes.

Apple Coffee Cake

Serve this gorgeous cake warm with ice cream or whipped cream.

◆ Base Recipe: package of Cake Mix, page 61	1	1
Apple juice	½ cup	125 mL
Vanilla	½ tsp.	2 mL
Small cooking apple (such as McIntosh), peeled, cored and diced	1	1
Chopped pecans (or walnuts)	⅓ cup	75 mL
Quick-cooking rolled oats (not instant)	¼ cup	60 mL
Brown sugar, packed	2 tbsp.	30 mL
Ground cinnamon	½ tsp.	2 mL
Hard margarine (or butter)	2 tbsp.	30 mL

Base Recipe: Thaw package of Cake Mix in medium bowl.

Add apple juice and vanilla. Beat on medium for 2 minutes until smooth. Spread in greased 9 inch (22 cm) round cake pan.

Sprinkle batter with apple and pecans.

Combine rolled oats, brown sugar and cinnamon in small bowl. Cut in margarine until mixture is crumbly. Sprinkle over apple. Bake in 350°F (175°C) oven for about 45 minutes. A wooden pick inserted in center should come out clean. Cuts into 8 wedges.

1 wedge: 364 Calories; 13.7 g Total Fat; 297 mg Sodium; 4 g Protein; 57 g Carbohydrate; 2 g Dietary Fiber

Pictured on page 107.

To Make Ahead: Bake early in day or night before.

To Freeze: Bake, cool and wrap. Label. Freeze for up to 3 months. To serve, see Tip, page 61.

Paré Pointer

A cat that has swallowed a duck is known as a duck-filled fatty puss.

Gingerbread Cake

Serve warm with whipped topping, ice cream or applesauce.

◆ Base Recipe: package of Cake Mix, page 61	1	1
Fancy (mild) molasses	⅓ cup	75 mL
Milk	⅓ cup	75 mL
Large egg	1	1
Ground ginger	1½ tsp.	7 mL
Ground cinnamon	¼ tsp.	1 mL
Ground cloves	⅟₁₆ tsp.	0.5 mL

Base Recipe: Thaw package of Cake Mix in medium bowl.

Add remaining 6 ingredients. Beat on medium for about 2 minutes until smooth. Spoon into greased 9 x 9 inch (22 x 22 cm) pan. Spread evenly. Bake in 350°F (175°C) oven for 40 minutes. A wooden pick inserted in center should come out clean. Cuts into 9 pieces.

1 piece: 269 Calories; 6.4 g Total Fat; 140 mg Sodium; 3 g Protein; 50 g Carbohydrate; 1 g Dietary Fiber

Pictured on page 125.

To Make Ahead: Bake early in day or night before.

To Freeze: Bake, cool and wrap. Label. Freeze for up to 3 months. To serve, see Tip, page 61.

Paré Pointer

Raining cats and dogs is bad enough but hailing taxis is worse.

Steak Parmesan

Cheesy tender steak with a spicy tomato sauce. Very delicious.

Fine dry bread crumbs	¼ cup	60 mL
Grated Parmesan cheese	¼ cup	60 mL
All-purpose flour	2 tbsp.	30 mL
Seasoned salt	½ tsp.	2 mL
Large egg	1	1
Boneless fast-fry sirloin steak, cut into 4 servings	1 lb.	454 g
SAUCE		
Cooking oil	1 tbsp.	15 mL
Chopped onion	1 cup	250 mL
All-purpose flour	2 tbsp.	30 mL
Can of tomato sauce	7½ oz.	213 mL
Ketchup	¼ cup	60 mL
Water	½ cup	125 mL
Dried whole oregano	½ tsp.	2 mL
Dried sweet basil	½ tsp.	2 mL
Granulated sugar	1 tsp.	5 mL
Salt	½ tsp.	2 mL
Pepper	¼ tsp.	1 mL
Cooking oil	1 tbsp.	15 mL
Grated part-skim mozzarella cheese	1½ cups	375 mL

Stir first 4 ingredients in shallow dish.

Break egg into separate shallow dish. Beat with fork. Dip each steak portion into beaten egg. Coat bread with crumb mixture. Set aside.

Sauce: Heat first amount of cooking oil in frying pan. Add onion. Sauté until soft.

(continued on next page)

Beef

Sprinkle flour over top. Mix well. Add tomato sauce, ketchup and water. Stir until boiling and thickened. Stir in oregano, basil, sugar, salt and pepper. Remove to small bowl to cool.

Heat second amount of cooking oil in same frying pan on medium-high. Brown steaks on both sides.

Arrange steaks in greased shallow casserole or 9 x 9 inch (22 x 22 cm) pan. Cover with sauce. Sprinkle with cheese. Bake, uncovered, in 425°F (220°C) oven for 10 minutes until hot and cheese is melted. Serves 4.

1 serving: 488 Calories; 24.6 g Total Fat; 1512 mg Sodium; 39 g Protein; 27 g Carbohydrate; 2 g Dietary Fiber

---

Prep Time: 25 minutes to coat and brown steak; 25 minutes to prepare sauce and heat steak with sauce in oven.

To Make Ahead: Assemble or bake early in day or night before. Cover. Chill. To serve, bake as above or reheat.

To Freeze: Assemble in casserole. Cover. Label. Freeze for up to 2 months. To serve, thaw, cover and heat in 350°F (175°C) oven for 30 minutes until cheese is melted.

Paré Pointer

That rooster is so lazy he waits for another rooster to crow and then he nods his head.

Steak Bake

Economical as well as being a make-ahead! Tender and tasty.

Cooking oil	1 tbsp.	15 mL
Round steak, trimmed of fat, cut into 8 pieces	2 lbs.	900 g
Cooking oil	1 tsp.	5 mL
Chopped onion	½ cup	125 mL
Ketchup (or chili sauce)	½ cup	125 mL
White vinegar	¼ cup	60 mL
Water	½ cup	125 mL
Apple juice (or water)	¼ cup	60 mL
Prepared mustard	1 tbsp.	15 mL
Worcestershire sauce	1½ tsp.	7 mL
Beef bouillon powder	1 tsp.	5 mL
Seasoned salt	½ tsp.	2 mL
Pepper	$\frac{1}{16}$ tsp.	0.5 mL

Heat first amount of cooking oil in frying pan. Add steak. Brown on both sides on medium-high. Transfer in single layer to small roaster.

Add second amount of cooking oil to frying pan. Add onion. Sauté until soft. Spoon over each portion of steak.

Mix remaining 9 ingredients in medium bowl. Pour slowly over each portion of steak. Bake, covered, in 300°F (150°C) oven for 2½ to 3 hours. Serves 8.

1 serving: 165 Calories; 5.1 g Total Fat; 455 mg Sodium; 22 g Protein; 8 g Carbohydrate; 1 g Dietary Fiber

Prep Time: 20 minutes to prepare and assemble.

To Make Ahead: Assemble or bake early in day or night before. Cover. Chill. To serve, bake as above or reheat.

To Freeze: Cover unbaked casserole. Label. Freeze for up to 2 months. To serve, thaw and bake as above. To bake from frozen state, see Tip, page 69.

Beef

Beefy Noodle Bake

This is a very cheesy casserole complemented by basil and oregano.

Medium noodles (about 4 cups, 1 L)	8 oz.	225 g
Boiling water	2½ qts.	2.5 L
Cooking oil (optional)	1 tbsp.	15 mL
Salt	2 tsp.	10 mL
Light creamed cottage cheese	2 cups	500 mL
Light cream cheese, cut up	4 oz.	125 g
Cooking oil	2 tsp.	10 mL
Lean ground beef	1 lb.	454 g
Chopped onion	1 cup	250 mL
Can of tomato sauce	14 oz.	398 mL
Granulated sugar	1 tsp.	5 mL
Dried sweet basil	¾ tsp.	4 mL
Salt	½ tsp.	2 mL
Pepper	¼ tsp.	1 mL
Garlic powder	⅛ tsp.	0.5 mL
Ground oregano	⅛ tsp.	0.5 mL

Cook noodles in boiling water and first amounts of cooking oil and salt in large uncovered pot or Dutch oven for 5 to 7 minutes until tender but firm. Drain. Turn into ungreased 3 quart (3 L) casserole.

Place cottage cheese in blender. Add cream cheese. Process, scraping down sides several times, until smooth. Pour over noodles.

Heat second amount of cooking oil in frying pan. Add ground beef and onion. Sauté until beef is browned. Drain.

Add remaining 7 ingredients. Stir. Spoon over top of cottage cheese mixture. Bake, uncovered, in 350°F (175°C) oven for 30 to 40 minutes. Serves 4.

1 serving: 590 Calories; 17.7 g Total Fat; 1758 mg Sodium; 48 g Protein; 59 g Carbohydrate; 3 g Dietary Fiber

Prep Time: 30 minutes to prepare and assemble.

To Make Ahead: Assemble or bake early in day or night before. Cover. Chill. To serve, bake as above or reheat.

To Freeze: Cover unbaked casserole. Label. Freeze for up to 2 months. To serve, thaw and bake as above. To bake from frozen state, see Tip, page 69.

Santa Fe Lasagne

Lasagne with a mild chili flavor makes this different from the usual.

Lasagna noodles	12	12
Boiling water	4 qts.	4 L
Cooking oil (optional)	1 tbsp.	15 mL
Salt	1 tbsp.	15 mL
MEAT SAUCE		
Cooking oil	2 tsp.	10 mL
Lean ground beef	1¼ lbs.	560 g
Chopped onion	¾ cup	175 mL
Chopped celery	⅓ cup	75 mL
Can of stewed tomatoes, with juice	14 oz.	398 mL
Cans of tomato sauce (7½ oz., 213 mL, each)	2	2
Can of diced green chilies, with juice	4 oz.	114 mL
Envelope taco seasoning mix	1¼ oz.	35 g
COTTAGE CHEESE SAUCE		
Light creamed cottage cheese	2 cups	500 mL
Large eggs	2	2
Grated Monterey Jack cheese	2 cups	500 mL

Cook noodles in boiling water, cooking oil and salt in large uncovered pot or Dutch oven for about 14 to 16 minutes until tender but firm. Drain. Set aside.

Meat Sauce: Heat cooking oil in frying pan. Add beef, onion and celery. Scramble-fry until lightly browned. Drain.

Stir in tomatoes with juice, tomato sauce, green chilies with juice and taco mix. Set aside.

(continued on next page)

Beef

Cottage Cheese Sauce: Mix cottage cheese and eggs well in medium bowl. Assemble ingredients in greased 9 × 13 inch (22 × 33 cm) pan or in two 8 × 8 inch (20 × 20 cm) pans for 2 meals as follows:

1. Small amount of meat sauce
2. $\frac{1}{3}$ of noodles
3. $\frac{1}{3}$ of meat sauce
4. $\frac{1}{2}$ of cottage cheese sauce
5. $\frac{1}{3}$ of noodles

6. $\frac{1}{3}$ of meat sauce
7. $\frac{1}{2}$ of cottage cheese sauce
8. $\frac{1}{3}$ of noodles
9. $\frac{1}{3}$ of meat sauce
10. All of Monterey Jack cheese

Bake, uncovered, in 350°F (175°C) oven for 1 hour. Let stand for 10 minutes before serving. Serves 6 to 8.

1 serving: 429 Calories; 18.1 g Total Fat; 1520 mg Sodium; 34 g Protein; 33 g Carbohydrate; 3 g Dietary Fiber

Prep Time: 1 hour to prepare and assemble—well worth the time!

To Make Ahead: Assemble or bake early in day or night before. Cover. Chill. To serve, bake as above or reheat.

To Freeze: Bake, cool and cover. Label. Freeze for up to 2 months. To bake from frozen state, see Tip, below.

Select-A-Meal: See page 12.

 To reheat a casserole in a Pyrex dish from the frozen state, place in cold oven and allow an extra 30 minutes baking time. Keep covered for the first cooking time and then uncover for the last 15 to 30 minutes. To check to see if casserole is heated through, place a knife blade into the center of the casserole to the bottom and hold for 10 seconds. Remove. Blade should be hot to the touch.

Beefy Chicken Loaf

*Made with lean ground beef and lean ground chicken, this
loaf has a mild smoky barbecue taste.*

Large egg, fork-beaten	1	1
Milk	¼ cup	60 mL
Salt	½ tsp.	2 mL
Seasoned salt	½ tsp.	2 mL
Pepper	¼ tsp.	1 mL
Worcestershire sauce	1 tbsp.	15 mL
Liquid smoke	¹⁄₁₆ tsp.	0.5 mL
Finely chopped onion	½ cup	125 mL
Lean ground beef	1 lb.	454 g
Lean ground chicken (or turkey)	½ lb.	225 g
Quick-cooking rolled oats (not instant)	¾ cup	175 mL
Ketchup	¼ cup	60 mL
Prepared mustard	1 tbsp.	15 mL
Brown sugar, packed	1 tbsp.	15 mL

Mix first 7 ingredients in large bowl.

Add next 4 ingredients. Mix well. Pack into greased 8 x 4 x 3 inch
(20 x 10 x 7.5 cm) loaf pan.

Combine remaining 3 ingredients in small dish. Spread over meatloaf.
Bake, uncovered, in 350°F (175°C) oven for about 1 hour. Serves 6.

*1 serving: 293 Calories; 13.7 g Total Fat; 639 mg Sodium; 27 g Protein; 15 g Carbohydrate;
2 g Dietary Fiber*

Prep Time: 10 minutes to prepare and assemble.

To Make Ahead: Assemble or bake early in day or night before. Cover. Chill.
To serve, bake as above or reheat.

To Freeze: Tightly wrap unbaked loaf. Label. Freeze for up to 3 months. To
serve, thaw and bake as above. To bake from frozen state, see Tip, page 69.

Select-A-Meal: See page 12.

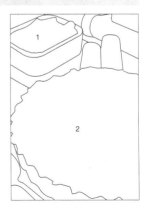

1. Crispy Cukes, page 122
2. Chicken Quiche, page 102

Props Courtesy Of: Le Gnome
                     The Bay

Individual Meatloaves

Horseradish gives a nice bite.

Large egg, fork-beaten	1	1
Water	⅓ cup	75 mL
Minced onion flakes (or ⅓ cup, 75 mL, finely chopped onion)	2 tbsp.	30 mL
Worcestershire sauce	1 tsp.	5 mL
Prepared horseradish	2 tsp.	10 mL
Ketchup (or chili sauce)	2 tbsp.	30 mL
Salt	1 tsp.	5 mL
Pepper	¼ tsp.	1 mL
Fine dry bread crumbs	⅓ cup	75 mL
Lean ground beef	1 lb.	454 g

Combine first 8 ingredients in medium bowl. Mix well.

Add bread crumbs. Stir until blended. Mix in ground beef. Divide into 4 equal portions. Shape each portion into small meatloaf. Arrange on greased baking sheet. Bake in 350°F (175°C) oven for 30 minutes. Drain. Makes 4 loaves.

1 loaf: 249 Calories; 11.1 g Total Fat; 928 mg Sodium; 24 g Protein; 13 g Carbohydrate; 1 g Dietary Fiber

---

Prep Time: 20 minutes to prepare and assemble.

To Make Ahead: Assemble or bake early in day or night before. Cover. Chill. To serve, bake as above or reheat.

To Freeze: Wrap unbaked loaves. Label. Freeze for up to 3 months. To serve, thaw and bake wrapped loaves as above.

Select-A-Meal: See page 12.

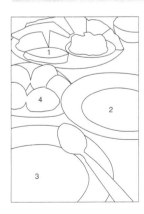

1. Seed And Cheese Wedges, page 59
2. Potato Cabbage Soup, page 132
3. Bean Soup, page 133
4. Fridge Buns, page 75

Props Courtesy Of: The Bay

Muffins-On-Hand

A wonderful way to have fresh muffins every morning.

Natural bran	3 cups	750 mL
All-bran cereal (100%)	4 cups	1 L
Boiling water	2 cups	500 mL
Buttermilk (or reconstituted from powder)	4 cups	1 L
Hard margarine (or butter), softened	1 cup	250 mL
Granulated sugar	2½ cups	625 mL
Large eggs	4	4
All-purpose flour	5 cups	1.25 L
Baking soda	1½ tbsp.	25 mL
Salt	1½ tsp.	7 mL

Measure bran and bran cereal into very large bowl. Add boiling water. Stir. Let stand for 10 minutes.

Add buttermilk. Stir.

Cream margarine and sugar in second bowl. Beat in eggs, 1 at a time, until smooth. Add to bran mixture. Stir.

Stir flour, baking soda and salt in large bowl to blend. Add to batter. Stir just to moisten. Turn into plastic pail. Cover. Chill. Keeps for 4 to 5 weeks in refrigerator. Fill greased muffin cups almost full. Bake in 400°F (205°C) oven for 15 to 20 minutes. A wooden pick inserted near center should come out clean. Makes 5 dozen muffins.

1 muffin: 133 Calories; 4.1 g Total Fat; 260 mg Sodium; 3 g Protein; 24 g Carbohydrate; 3 g Dietary Fiber

RAISIN MUFFINS-ON-HAND: Add 3 to 4 cups (750 mL to 1 L) raisins.

Prep Time: 20 minutes to prepare and assemble.

To Make Ahead: Bake shortly before serving or early in day.

To Freeze: Bake, cool and wrap. Label. Freeze for up to 3 months. To serve, see Tip, page 61.

Fridge Buns

Subtle molasses flavor in these yeasty buns.
Wonderful aroma as they bake. No kneading required.

Hard margarine (or butter), melted	½ cup	125 mL
Large egg	1	1
Warm water	1 cup	250 mL
Granulated sugar	¼ cup	60 mL
Fancy (mild) molasses	2 tbsp.	30 mL
Salt	½-¾ tsp.	2-4 mL
Whole wheat flour	1½ cups	375 mL
Instant yeast	2½ tsp.	12 mL
All-purpose flour (approximately)	2¼ cups	560 mL

Melt margarine in small saucepan. Pour into large bowl. Cool to lukewarm.

Add egg. Beat well.

Add next 4 ingredients. Beat to mix.

Add whole wheat flour and yeast. Beat for 2 minutes.

Gradually work in all-purpose flour until moistened. Shape into buns about 2 oz. (57 g) each. Arrange buns on greased baking sheet, 1 inch (2.5 cm) apart for crusty sides or close together for soft sides. Cover. Chill overnight. Cover with tea towel. Let rise in oven with light on and door closed for about 1 hour. They will rise more as they bake. Bake in 425°F (220°C) oven for about 15 minutes. Makes 18 buns.

1 bun: 166 Calories; 5.6 g Total Fat; 139 mg Sodium; 4 g Protein; 25 g Carbohydrate; 2 g Dietary Fiber

Pictured on page 72.

Prep Time: 15 minutes to prepare and shape buns.

To Make Ahead: Prepare night before. To serve, bake as above.

To Freeze: Arrange formed buns on baking sheet, not touching. Freeze, uncovered, for 2 hours. Remove buns to freezer bags. Label. Freeze for up to 3 months. To serve, cover with tea towel and thaw at room temperature for 1 hour. Still covered, let rise in oven with light on and door closed for 1 hour. Bake as above.

Freezer Biscuits

It's very handy to have these in the freezer to bake at a moment's notice.

All-purpose flour	6 cups	1.5 L
Skim milk powder	½ cup	125 mL
Granulated sugar	¼ cup	60 mL
Baking powder	¼ cup	60 mL
Cream of tartar	2 tsp.	10 mL
Salt	2 tsp.	10 mL
Hard margarine (or butter), cut up	1¼ cups	300 mL
Water	1¾ cups	425 mL

Measure first 6 ingredients into large bowl. Stir well. Cut in margarine with pastry cutter until mixture resembles coarse crumbs.

Add water. Stir until moistened enough to form a soft ball. Working with ½ of dough at a time, turn out onto lightly floured surface. Knead 8 to 10 times. Pat out dough to ¾ inch (2 cm) thickness. Cut, using round 3 inch (7 cm) cutter, pushing straight down. Gently rework scraps and repeat with remaining ½ of dough until all is used. Arrange frozen biscuits on ungreased baking sheet. Bake in center of 400°F (205°C) oven for 25 to 30 minutes until golden. Makes 48 biscuits.

1 biscuit: 117 Calories; 5.3 g Total Fat; 200 mg Sodium; 2 g Protein; 15 g Carbohydrate; 1 g Dietary Fiber

Pictured on page 17.

Prep Time: 20 minutes to prepare and shape biscuits.

To Make Ahead And Freeze: Arrange formed biscuits on baking sheet, not touching. Freeze, uncovered, for 2 hours. Remove biscuits to freezer bags. Label. Freeze for up to 3 months. To serve, bake as above.

Paré Pointer
*Don't run over birds with your lawn mower
or you'll end up with shredded tweet.*

Garlic Bread

Just enough garlic!

Margarine (or butter), softened	½ cup	125 mL
Garlic clove, minced (or ½ tsp., 2 mL, garlic salt)	1	1
French bread loaf, cut into 1 inch (2.5 cm) thick slices	1	1

Combine margarine and garlic in small bowl. Mix well.

Spread margarine mixture on both sides of each slice. Spread lightly at first to be sure of coverage. Divide any remaining mixture on slices. Keeping slices in order, reshape loaf on double layer of foil or single layer of heavy-duty foil. Wrap well. Bake in 350°F (175°C) oven for 20 minutes. Makes about 14 slices.

1 slice: 157 Calories; 8 g Total Fat; 270 mg Sodium; 3 g Protein; 18 g Carbohydrate; 1 g Dietary Fiber

HOT BUTTERED BREAD: Omit garlic. Bake as above.

GARLIC TOAST: Lay individual slices on ungreased baking sheet. Broil each side for about 4 minutes.

Prep Time: 10 minutes to prepare and assemble.

To Make Ahead: Assemble early in day or night before. Chill. To serve, bake as above.

To Freeze: Wrap unbaked loaf. Label. Freeze for up to 3 months. To serve, thaw and bake as above. To bake from frozen state, double baking time to 40 minutes.

 tip

To make croutons from the leftover Garlic Bread (above), cut French bread into 1 inch (2.5 cm) cubes; place in a shallow baking pan. Drizzle with olive oil or melted butter and toss. Bake at 350°F (175°C) for 20 minutes or until gold and crisp. Store in a tightly sealed container.

Cordon Bleu Roll

Yummy, wonderful and mellow variation. Once cut, a pinwheel look is revealed. Serve with Mushroom Sauce, page 31.

CHICKEN LAYER

Large egg, fork-beaten	1	1
Onion flakes	1 tsp.	5 mL
Chicken bouillon powder	2 tsp.	10 mL
Milk	½ cup	125 mL
Fine dry bread crumbs	½ cup	125 mL
Salt	½ tsp.	2 mL
Pepper	½ tsp.	2 mL
Lean ground chicken	1½ lbs.	680 g

FILLING

Light process Cheddar (or Swiss) cheese slices	6	6
Fat-free ham slices	6	6

Chicken Layer: Stir first 7 ingredients in large bowl.

Add ground chicken. Mix well. Press out on foil to 8 x 10 inch (20 x 25 cm) rectangle.

Filling: Cover chicken mixture with cheese. Lay ham slices evenly over cheese. Roll up from short side, using foil to assist in rolling. Discard foil. Press ends and seam of chicken mixture to prevent cheese from oozing out. Place, seam side down, on greased baking sheet. Bake in 350°F (175°C) oven for 1 to 1¼ hours until browned and chicken is cooked in center of roll. Serves 6.

1 serving: 247 Calories; 4.5 g Total Fat; 1190 mg Sodium; 37 g Protein; 12 g Carbohydrate; trace Dietary Fiber

Pictured on page 144.

Prep Time: 20 minutes to prepare and assemble. **To Make Ahead:** Assemble or bake early in day or night before. Cover. Chill. To serve, bake as above or reheat.

To Freeze: Wrap unbaked chicken roll. Label. Freeze for up to 2 months. To serve, thaw and bake as above.

Select-A-Meal: See page 12.

Chicken Pecan

The toasted nut crust makes these moist inside and quite delicious.

Boneless, skinless chicken breast halves (about 1 lb., 454 g)	4	4
Cooking oil	2 tsp.	10 mL
Prepared mustard	1 tsp.	5 mL
Prepared horseradish	1/2 tsp.	2 mL
Ground pecans	1 cup	250 mL
Salt	1/2 tsp.	2 mL
Pepper	1/8 tsp.	0.5 mL
Cooking oil	1 tbsp.	15 mL
Margarine (or butter)	1 tbsp.	15 mL

Pound chicken to 1/2 inch (12 mm) thickness.

Stir first amount of cooking oil, mustard and horseradish in small cup. Brush chicken with mustard mixture.

Stir pecans, salt and pepper in shallow dish. Press chicken into pecan mixture to coat completely.

Heat second amount of cooking oil and margarine in non-stick frying pan. Add chicken. Cook both sides on medium for about 4 minutes per side until browned and no pink remains. Serves 4.

1 serving: 376 Calories; 27.2 g Total Fat; 470 mg Sodium; 29 g Protein; 5 g Carbohydrate; 2 g Dietary Fiber

Prep Time: 20 minutes includes grinding pecans.

To Make Ahead: Assemble or cook early in day or night before. Cover. Chill. To serve, cook as above or reheat.

To Freeze: Cover uncooked chicken. Label. Freeze for up to 4 months. To serve, thaw and bake as above.

Select-A-Meal: See page 12.

Paré Pointer

Of course you know why cows wear bells. Their horns don't work!

Chicken Pasta Casserole

So nice to be able to have this all ready to pop in the oven. Very flavorful.

Fettuccine (or other pasta)	8 oz.	225 g
Boiling water	2½ qts.	2.5 L
Cooking oil (optional)	1 tbsp.	15 mL
Salt	2 tsp.	10 mL
Boneless, skinless chicken breast halves (about 4), not previously frozen, cut bite size	1 lb.	454 g
Chopped onion	½ cup	125 mL
Chopped green pepper	⅓ cup	75 mL
Cooking oil	1 tbsp.	15 mL
Chicken bouillon powder	2 tsp.	10 mL
Hot water	⅔ cup	150 mL
Can of condensed cream of mushroom soup	10 oz.	284 mL
Salt	¼ tsp.	1 mL
Pepper	½ tsp.	2 mL
Grated light sharp Cheddar cheese	½ cup	125 mL
Grated light sharp Cheddar cheese	½ cup	125 mL

Cook fettuccine in boiling water and first amounts of cooking oil and salt in large uncovered pot or Dutch oven for 9 to 11 minutes until tender but firm. Drain. Return fettuccine to pot.

Sauté chicken, onion and green pepper in second amount of cooking oil in frying pan for about 6 minutes until chicken is golden. Stir into fettuccine.

Stir bouillon powder into hot water in medium bowl to dissolve. Mix in soup, second amount of salt, pepper and first amount of cheese. Add to pasta mixture. Stir gently. Turn into ungreased 2 quart (2 L) casserole.

Sprinkle with second amount of cheese. Bake, uncovered, in 350°F (175°C) oven for 40 to 45 minutes until heated through. Serves 4.

1 serving: 548 Calories; 17.7 g Total Fat; 1375 mg Sodium; 43 g Protein; 51 g Carbohydrate; 2 g Dietary Fiber

Prep Time: 30 minutes to prepare and assemble.

To Make Ahead: Assemble or bake early in day or night before. Cover. Chill. To serve, bake as above or reheat.

To Freeze: Cover unbaked casserole. Label. Freeze for up to 2 months. To serve, thaw and bake as above. To bake from frozen state, see Tip, page 69.

Baked Chicken Sandwich

The corn flake coating on these is crispy without deep-frying.

Boneless, skinless chicken breasts (about 4), very finely chopped	1 lb.	454 g
Cooking oil	1 tbsp.	15 mL
All-purpose flour	1 tbsp.	15 mL
Salt	1/2 tsp.	2 mL
Pepper	1/8 tsp.	0.5 mL
Onion powder	1/4 tsp.	1 mL
Chicken bouillon powder	1/2 tsp.	2 mL
Cayenne pepper (optional)	1/8 tsp.	0.5 mL
Milk	3/4 cup	175 mL
Margarine (or butter)	1/3 cup	75 mL
Whole wheat (or white) bread slices, crusts removed	16	16
Large eggs	4	4
Water	1/4 cup	60 mL
Crushed corn flakes cereal	2 cups	500 mL

Sauté chopped chicken in cooking oil in frying pan until no pink remains.

Mix in flour, salt, pepper, onion powder, chicken bouillon powder and cayenne pepper. Stir in milk until boiling and thickened. Cool.

Spread margarine on 1 side of each bread slice. Divide and spread filling over 8 slices. Cover with remaining 8 slices to make 8 sandwiches. Cut each sandwich in half.

Beat eggs and water in shallow bowl until smooth. Dip sandwiches in egg, then roll in cereal. Arrange on greased baking sheet. Bake in 325°F (160°C) oven for about 30 minutes until browned. Makes 8 sandwiches.

1 sandwich: 379 Calories; 10.5 g Total Fat; 848 mg Sodium; 24 g Protein; 49 g Carbohydrate; 4 g Dietary Fiber

Pictured on page 89.

Prep Time: 25 minutes to dipping stage.

To Make Ahead: Prepare filling early in day or night before. Cover. Chill. To serve, assemble, dip and bake as above.

To Freeze: Assemble sandwiches, not dipping into egg mixture. Wrap individual sandwiches. Label. Freeze for up to 2 months. To serve, thaw, dip, coat and bake as above.

Chicken Bombay

This tender chicken dish has a mild and slightly sweet curry flavor.

Margarine (or butter)	¼ cup	60 mL
Prepared mustard	¼ cup	60 mL
Liquid honey	½ cup	125 mL
Seasoned salt	½ tsp.	2 mL
Chili powder	¼ tsp.	1 mL
Onion powder	¼ tsp.	1 mL
Curry powder	¼ tsp.	1 mL
Salt	½ tsp.	2 mL
Pepper	¼ tsp.	1 mL
Chicken parts, bone in, skin removed, patted dry with paper towel	3 lbs.	1.4 kg

Mix first 9 ingredients in small saucepan. Heat and stir to liquefy.

Roll each part of chicken in sauce. Place in single layer in greased 9 x 13 inch (22 x 33 cm) pan. Bake, uncovered, in 375°F (190°C) oven for about 1 hour until tender, spooning on any remaining sauce at half-time. Serves 4.

1 serving: 456 Calories; 17.9 g Total Fat; 996 mg Sodium; 37 g Protein; 38 g Carbohydrate; 1 g Dietary Fiber

Pictured on front cover.

Prep Time: 25 to 30 minutes including removing skin. Or 8 to 10 minutes if beginning with skinless chicken.

To Make Ahead: Assemble early in day or night before. Cover. Chill. To serve, bake as above.

To Freeze: Cover baked casserole. Label. Freeze for up to 4 months. To serve, thaw and bake as above. To serve from frozen state, see Tip, page 69.

Paré Pointer
Ghosts use skeleton keys to open locked doors.

Turkey Schnitzel

Keep lots of these on hand in the freezer.
They only take 10 to 15 minutes to brown and cook.

All-purpose flour	½ cup	125 mL
Large eggs, fork-beaten	2	2
Water	2 tbsp.	30 mL
Fine dry bread crumbs	1 cup	250 mL
Seasoned salt	1 tsp.	5 mL
Pepper	½ tsp.	2 mL
Paprika	2 tsp.	10 mL
Garlic powder (optional)	¼ tsp.	1 mL
Turkey cutlets (about 8), pounded thin	2 lbs.	900 g
Margarine (or butter)	2 tbsp.	30 mL

Spread flour on saucer. Set aside.

Beat eggs and water with fork in small bowl until smooth.

Combine bread crumbs, seasoned salt, pepper, paprika and garlic powder in medium bowl.

Dip cutlets, 1 at a time, into flour to coat. Dip into egg mixture. Coat with crumb mixture. Dry on waxed paper-lined baking sheet in refrigerator for 30 minutes.

Heat margarine in frying pan on medium-high. Add cutlets, browning both sides. Reduce heat. Cover. Cook for 10 to 15 minutes until no pink remains in turkey. Serves 8.

1 serving: 261 Calories; 6.9 g Total Fat; 734 mg Sodium; 30 g Protein; 18 g Carbohydrate; 1 g Dietary Fiber

Pictured on page 126.

Prep Time: 10 minutes to prepare and assemble.

To Make Ahead: Assemble early in day or night before. Cover. Chill. To serve, brown and cook as above.

To Freeze: If freezing before frying, use fresh turkey. Wrap uncooked individual portions. Label. Freeze for up to 4 months. To serve, thaw and cook as above.

Select-A-Meal: See page 12.

Chewy Chocolate Cookies

A great chocolate fix! Lots of chocolate chips in a brownie-like cookie.

Hard margarine (or butter), softened	1 cup	250 mL
Granulated sugar	1 cup	250 mL
Large eggs	2	2
Vanilla	2 tsp.	10 mL
All-purpose flour	2 cups	500 mL
Cocoa, sifted if lumpy	¾ cup	175 mL
Baking soda	1 tsp.	5 mL
Salt	½ tsp.	2 mL
Semisweet chocolate chips	2 cups	500 mL

Cream margarine and sugar in large bowl. Beat in eggs, 1 at a time. Add vanilla. Beat well.

Stir flour, cocoa, baking soda and salt in medium bowl. Gradually stir into batter.

Stir in chocolate chips. Roll into 1 inch (2.5 cm) balls. Place on ungreased cookie sheet. Flatten slightly with bottom of glass. Bake in 350°F (175°C) oven for 10 minutes. Let stand for 3 minutes before removing. Makes about 4 dozen cookies.

1 cookie: 111 Calories; 6.6 g Total Fat; 108 mg Sodium; 1 g Protein; 13 g Carbohydrate; 1 g Dietary Fiber

Prep Time: 25 minutes to prepare and shape cookies.

To Make Ahead And Freeze: Arrange balls on cookie sheet, not touching. Freeze, uncovered, for 2 hours. Remove balls to freezer container. Label. Freeze for up to 6 months. To bake from frozen state, thaw on ungreased cookie sheet 1 inch (2.5 cm) apart for 10 to 15 minutes. Flatten and bake as above.

 tip

For even baking and browning, bake cookies in the center of the oven. If your oven has uneven heat distribution, you will find that the back row will bake and brown faster than those closer to the front. If so, turn the cookie sheet around halfway through the baking time. Also, if the bottoms of your cookies get too brown, raise the pan in the oven. If tops get too brown, lower the pan.

Peanut Butter Cookies

This could be the best peanut butter cookie you'll ever eat!
Slice and bake anytime the urge hits.

All-purpose flour	3 cups	750 mL
Granulated sugar	1 cup	250 mL
Baking soda	1 tsp.	5 mL
Salt	½ tsp.	2 mL
Hard margarine (or butter), softened	1 cup	250 mL
Smooth peanut butter	1 cup	250 mL
Golden corn syrup	½ cup	125 mL
Milk	2 tbsp.	30 mL

Stir flour, sugar, baking soda and salt in large bowl.

Mix in margarine and peanut butter until consistency of coarse meal.

Stir in corn syrup and milk. Shape into 4 rolls about 1½ inches (3.8 cm) in diameter. Cover dough with waxed paper in airtight container. Chill for 1 hour. Cut into ¼ inch (6 mm) slices. Place on ungreased baking sheet. Bake in 350°F (175°C) oven for about 14 minutes. Makes 8 dozen cookies.

1 cookie: 64 Calories; 3.5 g Total Fat; 67 mg Sodium; 1 g Protein; 7 g Carbohydrate; trace Dietary Fiber

FILLED PEANUT BUTTER COOKIES: Slice cookies as above but a bit thinner. Place ½ tsp. (2 mL) peanut butter and/or 3 chocolate chips in center of each unbaked cookie. Top with a second unbaked cookie. Press all around with a fork to seal. Bake as above.

Prep Time: 15 minutes to prepare and shape rolls.

To Make Ahead: Wrap rolls of dough in waxed paper. Can be baked later in day or next day.

To Freeze: Place rolls of dough in sealable plastic freezer bag. Label. Freeze for up to 6 months. To bake from frozen state, partially thaw to slice dough. Bake as above.

Iced Moments

This tender cookie is good with or without icing.
Like chocolate shortbread. Recipe is easy to double.

Hard margarine (or butter), softened	1 cup	250 mL
Icing (confectioner's) sugar	⅓ cup	75 mL
Cocoa	3 tbsp.	50 mL
Cornstarch	½ cup	125 mL
All-purpose flour	1½ cups	375 mL
Vanilla	1 tsp.	5 mL
ICING		
Hard margarine (or butter)	2 tbsp.	30 mL
Frozen concentrated orange juice	4 tsp.	20 mL
Lemon juice	1 tsp.	5 mL
Icing (confectioner's) sugar	½ cup	125 mL

Work all 6 ingredients together well in large bowl. Knead to form ball of dough. Shape into 2 rolls 1¾ inches (4.5 cm) in diameter. Wrap dough in waxed paper. Chill for 1 hour. Cut chilled dough into ¼ inch (6 mm) slices. Place on ungreased baking sheet. Bake in 325°F (160°C) oven for 15 to 18 minutes. Cool.

Icing: Melt margarine and concentrated orange juice in small saucepan. Mix in lemon juice and icing sugar. Dip cookie tops in glaze, allowing excess to drip off. Place cookies on waxed paper or plate to dry. Dries to a fairly hard, glossy finish. Makes 3 dozen cookies.

1 cookie: 95 Calories; 6.2 g Total Fat; 71 mg Sodium; 1 g Protein; 9 g Carbohydrate; trace Dietary Fiber

Pictured on page 89.

Prep Time: 10 minutes to prepare and shape rolls.

To Make Ahead: Wrap rolls of dough in waxed paper. Bake later in day or next day.

To Freeze: Place rolls of dough in sealable plastic freezer bag. Label. Freeze for up to 6 months. To bake from frozen state, partially thaw to slice dough. Bake as above.

Cookies

Chocolate Cinnamon Cookies

Makes a big batch.

Brown sugar, packed	1½ cups	375 mL
Hard margarine (or butter)	1½ cups	375 mL
Large eggs	2	2
All-purpose flour	4 cups	1 L
Cocoa	3 tbsp.	50 mL
Ground cinnamon	4 tsp.	20 mL
Baking soda	1 tsp.	5 mL
Salt	1 tsp.	5 mL
Chopped nuts	1 cup	250 mL

Beat brown sugar and margarine in large bowl. Add eggs, 1 at a time, beating well after each addition.

Stir flour, cocoa, cinnamon, baking soda and salt in medium bowl. Gradually add to batter, ⅓ at a time, beating slowly until well combined. Last ⅓ should be stirred in by hand as batter will be very stiff.

Stir in nuts. Divide dough into 4 portions. Shape each portion into roll about 2¼ inches (5.7 cm) in diameter. Wrap dough in waxed paper. Chill for 1 hour. Cut chilled dough into ¼ inch (6 mm) slices. Place on greased baking sheet. Bake in 350°F (175°C) oven for 10 minutes. Makes 8 dozen cookies.

1 cookie: 72 Calories; 4.1 g Total Fat; 81 mg Sodium; 1 g Protein; 8 g Carbohydrate; trace Dietary Fiber

---

Prep Time: 10 minutes to prepare and shape rolls.

To Make Ahead: Wrap rolls of dough in waxed paper. Bake later in day or next day.

To Freeze: Place rolls of dough in sealable plastic freezer bag. Label. Freeze for up to 6 months. To bake from frozen state, partially thaw to slice dough. Bake as above.

 tip   *If your frozen chocolate icing turns cloudy and whitish, it means that the chocolate has formed a "bloom." To restore, brush very lightly with cooking oil and let stand for two to three hours.*

Chocolate Bar Squares

Chewy coconut and chocolate in a quick and easy recipe.

Hard margarine (or butter)	¼ cup	60 mL
Can of sweetened condensed milk	11 oz.	300 mL
Fine or medium coconut	2 cups	500 mL
Chocolate cookie crumbs	2 cups	500 mL
TOPPING		
Cooking oil	1 tbsp.	15 mL
Milk chocolate chips	1 cup	250 mL

Melt margarine in large saucepan. Remove from heat. Stir in condensed milk.

Add coconut and cookie crumbs. Mix well. Pack into greased 9 x 9 inch (22 x 22 cm) pan. Bake in 350°F (175°C) oven for 10 to 13 minutes. Cool thoroughly.

Topping: Combine cooking oil and chocolate chips in small saucepan. Heat on low, stirring often, until smooth. Spread over bottom layer. Chill. Cuts into 48 squares.

1 square: 101 Calories; 6.4 g Total Fat; 31 mg Sodium; 1 g Protein; 11 g Carbohydrate; 1 g Dietary Fiber

Prep Time: 5 minutes to assemble.

To Make Ahead: Bake early in day or night before.

To Freeze: Cut squares. Place in freezer container. Cover. Label. Freeze for up to 2 months. See Tip, page 87. To serve, thaw.

1. Iced Moments, page 86
2. Stuffed Tomato Salad, page 121
3. Baked Chicken Sandwich, page 81

Props Courtesy Of: Chintz & Company
The Bay

Poppy Seed Cake

Ideal when someone drops in for coffee. Also good as a snack or dessert.

White cake mix, 2 layer size	1	1
Instant lemon pudding powder, 4 serving size	1	1
Poppy seeds	¼ cup	60 mL
Large eggs	4	4
Cooking oil	½ cup	125 mL
Water	1 cup	250 mL
GLAZE		
Lemon juice	1 tbsp.	15 mL
Icing (confectioner's) sugar	1 cup	250 mL

Put first 6 ingredients into large bowl. Beat on medium for about 2 minutes. Pour into greased and floured 12 cup (2.7 L) bundt pan. Bake in 350°F (175°C) oven for 45 to 50 minutes. A wooden pick inserted near center should come out clean. Cool for 15 minutes before turning out of pan to cool completely.

Glaze: Mix lemon juice and icing sugar in small bowl, adding more icing sugar or lemon juice as needed to make barely pourable glaze. Spoon over top of cake, allowing some to run down sides. Cuts into 16 pieces.

1 piece: 289 Calories; 13.3 g Total Fat; 156 mg Sodium; 3 g Protein; 40 g Carbohydrate; trace Dietary Fiber

Prep Time: 5 minutes to make batter; 5 minutes to make icing.

To Make Ahead: Make early in day or night before.

To Freeze: Wrap unglazed cake with plastic wrap, then wrap with foil and place in plastic freezer bag or freezer container. Label. Freeze for up to 4 months. To serve, thaw in wrapping. Prepare glaze and ice as above.

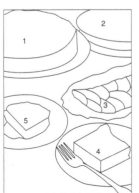

1. Dried Fruit Cheese Cake, page 97
2. Jiffy Pie, page 98
3. Fruit Strudel, page 96
4. Frozen Pumpkin Dessert, page 95
5. Ice Cream Toffee Slice, page 93

Props Courtesy Of: Stokes
The Bay

Praline Pecan Cake

A taste from the Deep South. Crunchy, sweet topping.

Yellow cake mix, 2 layer size	1	1
Instant vanilla pudding powder, 4 serving size	1	1
Water	1¼ cups	300 mL
Cooking oil	2 tbsp.	30 mL
Egg whites (large), room temperature	4	4
TOPPING		
Hard margarine (or butter)	⅓ cup	75 mL
Brown sugar, packed	1 cup	250 mL
Skim evaporated milk	¼ cup	60 mL
Chopped pecans	¾ cup	175 mL
Flake coconut	¼ cup	60 mL

Combine first 5 ingredients in large bowl until cake mix is moistened. Beat on medium for 2 minutes until smooth. Turn into greased 9 × 13 inch (22 × 33 cm) pan. Bake in 350°F (175°C) oven for about 35 minutes. A wooden pick inserted in center should come out clean. Cool.

Topping: Melt margarine in small saucepan. Stir in brown sugar until dissolved. Gradually stir in evaporated milk until mixture is smooth and starting to bubble. Stir in pecans and coconut. Spread over cooled cake. Broil on center rack in oven until topping is bubbly and golden. Watch carefully as it will burn easily. Cool. Cuts into 15 pieces.

1 piece: 348 Calories; 15.8 g Total Fat; 234 mg Sodium; 3 g Protein; 50 g Carbohydrate; 1 g Dietary Fiber

Prep Time: 5 minutes to mix batter; 5 minutes to make topping.

To Make Ahead: Make early in day or night before.

To Freeze: Wrap cake (without topping) with plastic wrap, then wrap with foil, place in plastic freezer bag or freezer container. Label. Freeze for up to 4 months. To serve, thaw in wrapping. Prepare topping as above.

 tip   *To prevent dried fruit from settling to the bottom of your cake, coat the fruit with a light dusting of flour before mixing into the batter.*

Ice Cream Toffee Slice

This dessert has chocolate crumbs top and bottom.
The sundae topping oozes out once dessert is cut.

CRUST		
Hard margarine (or butter)	³/₄ cup	175 mL
Chocolate wafer crumbs	2¹/₂ cups	625 mL
Granulated sugar	¹/₄ cup	60 mL

FILLING		
Vanilla ice cream (a rectangular block works best), cut into ³/₄ inch (2 cm) slices	2 qts.	2 L
Butterscotch (or caramel) sundae topping	1 cup	250 mL
Frozen light whipped topping, thawed, for garnish	1 cup	250 mL

Crust: Melt margarine in medium saucepan. Stir in wafer crumbs and sugar. Measure 1 cup (250 mL) crumbs and set aside. Press remaining crumbs evenly in bottom of ungreased 9 x 13 inch (22 x 33 cm) pan.

Filling: Place ice cream slices in single layer over crumb crust, cutting to fit. Sprinkle ice cream with ¹/₂ of reserved crumb mixture.

Drizzle butterscotch topping over top. Sprinkle with remaining ¹/₂ of crumb mixture, reserving about 2 tbsp. (30 mL) for final garnish. Freeze until firm.

Spread or pipe whipped topping over before serving. Sprinkle with reserved wafer crumbs. Cuts into 15 pieces.

1 piece: 392 Calories; 21.6 g Total Fat; 208 mg Sodium; 4 g Protein; 47 g Carbohydrate; trace Dietary Fiber

Pictured on page 90.

Prep Time: 20 minutes to assemble.

To Make Ahead And Freeze: Must be made early in day or night before. Cover ungarnished dessert. Label. Freeze for up to 4 months. To serve, garnish as above.

Apricot Smooch

Light and fluffy.

FIRST LAYER		
Hard margarine (or butter)	¼ cup	60 mL
Vanilla wafer crumbs	1 cup	250 mL
SECOND LAYER		
Hard margarine (or butter), softened	½ cup	125 mL
Icing (confectioner's) sugar	¾ cup	175 mL
Large egg	1	1
Almond flavoring	½ tsp.	2 mL
Vanilla	¼ tsp.	1 mL
THIRD LAYER		
Strained apricots (baby food), 4½ oz. (128 mL) each	2	2
FOURTH LAYER		
Frozen light whipped topping, thawed	2 cups	500 mL
Granulated sugar	1 tbsp.	15 mL
Almond flavoring	¼ tsp.	1 mL
Vanilla	¼ tsp.	1 mL
TOPPING		
Finely chopped pecans (or walnuts)	2 tbsp.	30 mL

First Layer: Melt margarine in small saucepan. Stir in wafer crumbs. Reserve 2 tbsp. (30 mL) for topping. Press remaining crumbs in ungreased 8 x 8 inch (20 x 20 cm) pan.

Second Layer: Put all 5 ingredients into small bowl. Beat until fluffy. Spread over first layer.

Third Layer: Spoon dabs of apricots randomly over second layer. Spread as evenly as possible.

Fourth Layer: Fold whipped topping, sugar and flavorings together in small bowl. Spread over third layer.

Topping: Mix reserved crumbs and pecans in small bowl. Sprinkle over fourth layer. Cuts into 9 pieces.

1 piece: 323 Calories; 21.6 g Total Fat; 293 mg Sodium; 2 g Protein; 32 g Carbohydrate; 1 g Dietary Fiber

Prep Time: 30 minutes to prepare and assemble.

To Make Ahead: Make early in day or up to 2 days before. Chill.

To Freeze: Do not garnish. Cover. Label. Freeze for up to 2 months. To serve, remove from freezer 30 minutes before serving. Garnish as above.

Frozen Pumpkin Dessert

A crunchy ginger base with a creamy pumpkin topping.

CRUST		
Hard margarine (or butter)	¼ cup	60 mL
Gingersnap cookie crumbs	1¾ cups	425 mL

FILLING		
Can of pumpkin (without spices)	14 oz.	398 mL
Brown sugar, packed	½ cup	125 mL
Granulated sugar	¼ cup	60 mL
Ground cinnamon	¾ tsp.	4 mL
Ground nutmeg	½ tsp.	2 mL
Ground ginger	½ tsp.	2 mL
Ground cloves	⅛ tsp.	0.5 mL
Salt	½ tsp.	2 mL
Vanilla ice cream, softened	1 qt.	1 L
Frozen light whipped topping, thawed, for garnish	1 cup	250 mL

Crust: Melt margarine in saucepan. Stir in cookie crumbs. Press in 9 x 9 inch (22 x 22 cm) pan. Bake in 350°F (175°C) oven for 10 minutes. Cool.

Filling: Mix first 8 ingredients in large bowl. Fold in ice cream. Spread evenly over crust. Freeze.

Remove from freezer 10 minutes before serving. Garnish with dollop of whipped topping. Cuts into 9 pieces.

1 piece: 336 Calories; 13.9 g Total Fat; 375 mg Sodium; 4 g Protein; 51 g Carbohydrate; 1 g Dietary Fiber

Pictured on page 90.

Prep Time: 15 minutes to prepare and assemble.

To Make Ahead And Freeze: Must be made early in day or night before. Do not garnish. Cover. Label. Freeze for up to 2 months. To serve, remove from freezer 10 minutes before serving. Garnish as above.

Fruit Strudel

Good fruit flavor. Slice and serve cold or warm with ice cream.

Chopped fresh fruit (or frozen fruit, thawed and drained)	2 cups	500 mL
Granulated sugar	2 tbsp.	30 mL
All-purpose flour	1¼ cups	300 mL
Salt	¼ tsp.	1 mL
Hard margarine (or butter)	½ cup	125 mL
Light sour cream	½ cup	125 mL
Light cream cheese	4 oz.	125 g
Almond flavoring	½ tsp.	2 mL
Slivered or sliced almonds, toasted	¼ cup	60 mL

Granulated sugar, for garnish

Combine fruit and sugar in small saucepan on medium. Stir. Heat for 10 minutes until soft and reduced to about half. Cool.

Measure flour and salt into medium bowl. Cut in margarine until crumbly.

Add sour cream. Mix well. Divide into 2 equal portions. Cover with plastic wrap. Chill. Roll out 1 portion on lightly floured surface to 12 x 15 inch (30 x 38 cm) rectangle.

Beat cream cheese and flavoring in small bowl. Spread ½ of cream cheese mixture in 4 inch (10 cm) lengthwise row down center of rectangle.

Spread ½ of fruit mixture over cream cheese layer. Sprinkle with ½ of almonds. Cut both sides of uncovered pastry in ¾ inch (2 cm) slices at a slight angle from edge of cream cheese layer to edge of pastry. Fold each strip alternately over fruit layer, creating a braided look. Repeat to make second braid. Transfer to greased baking sheet. Bake in 350°F (175°C) oven for 30 to 35 minutes until golden.

Sprinkle with sugar during last 10 minutes of baking. Cuts into 8 pieces.

1 piece: 273 Calories; 18.3 g Total Fat; 372 mg Sodium; 5 g Protein; 23 g Carbohydrate; 1 g Dietary Fiber

Pictured on page 90.

Prep Time: 40 minutes to prepare and assemble, including cooling time.

To Make Ahead: Bake early in day or night before.

To Freeze: Wrap baked strudel. Label. Freeze for up to 2 months. To serve, unwrap and thaw. Heat as above for 15 to 20 minutes until warm.

Dried Fruit Cheese Cake

Moist, rich texture with lots of golden fruit. Neither traditional cheesecake nor traditional fruitcake—but the best of both!

Chopped dried apricots	3/4 cup	175 mL
Light raisins	3/4 cup	175 mL
Granulated sugar	1/4 cup	60 mL
Water	2 cups	500 mL
Cream cheese, softened	8 oz.	250 g
Hard margarine (or butter), softened	1 cup	250 mL
Granulated sugar	1 1/2 cups	375 mL
Vanilla	1 1/2 tsp.	7 mL
Large eggs	4	4
All-purpose flour	2 cups	500 mL
Baking powder	1 1/2 tsp.	7 mL

Combine first 4 ingredients in medium saucepan. Bring to a boil. Simmer for 15 minutes. Drain well. Cool.

Beat cream cheese, margarine, sugar and vanilla in large bowl until smooth. Beat in eggs, 1 at a time, just to mix.

Stir in flour and baking powder. Stir in drained fruit. Turn into greased 10 inch (25 cm) springform pan. Bake in 350°F (175°C) oven for about 1 1/2 hours. Cuts into 16 pieces.

1 piece: 365 Calories; 18.6 g Total Fat; 204 mg Sodium; 5 g Protein; 46 g Carbohydrate; 1 g Dietary Fiber

Pictured on page 90.

Prep Time: 35 minutes to prepare and assemble.

To Make Ahead: Bake early in day or night before.

To Freeze: Wrap with plastic wrap or foil. Label. Freeze for up to 2 months. To serve, thaw in wrapping for 2 to 3 hours.

Jiffy Pie

A quick and light dessert! Fresh taste with a mousse-like texture.
Substitute any instant pudding flavor for a different taste.

CRUST		
Hard margarine (or butter)	⅓ cup	75 mL
Brown sugar, packed	3 tbsp.	50 mL
Graham cracker crumbs	1¼ cups	300 mL

FILLING		
Light cream cheese, softened	8 oz.	250 g
Milk	1 cup	250 mL
Instant lemon pudding powder, 4 serving size	1	1
Grated lemon peel (optional)	1 tsp.	5 mL
Frozen light whipped topping, thawed	2 cups	500 mL

Crust: Melt margarine in medium saucepan. Stir in brown sugar and graham crumbs. Reserve 3 tbsp. (50 mL). Press remaining crumbs into 9 inch (22 cm) pie plate, covering sides and bottom. Bake in 350°F (175°C) oven for 10 minutes. Cool.

Filling: Beat cream cheese and milk in large bowl until smooth. Add pudding powder and lemon peel. Beat well. Fold in whipped topping. Pour into pie shell. Sprinkle with reserved crumbs. Chill for at least 2 hours. Cuts into 8 wedges.

1 wedge: 350 Calories; 19.9 g Total Fat; 548 mg Sodium; 6 g Protein; 40 g Carbohydrate; trace Dietary Fiber

Pictured on page 90.

Prep Time: 15 minutes to prepare and bake pie shell; 10 minutes to prepare filling.

To Make Ahead: Must be made at least 2 hours in advance and can be made the day before. Prepare pie shell up to 3 days ahead. Do not freeze.

 Don't have graham crumbs on hand, only the graham crackers? Place the crackers into a large plastic freezer bag and seal closed. Use a rolling pin to roll back and forth over the crackers until they are the desired crumb consistency.

Peach Pie

Fresh peach flavor is a little bit of summer to savor.

Granulated sugar	1 cup	250 mL
Cornstarch	1/4 cup	60 mL
Water	1 cup	250 mL
Corn syrup	2 tbsp.	30 mL
Lemon juice	1 tsp.	5 mL
Package peach-flavored gelatin (jelly powder)	3 oz.	85 g
Fresh peaches (about 4), peeled, cut into slices, then each cut into 4 pieces	3 cups	750 mL
Baked 9 inch (22 cm) pie shell	1	1
Frozen light whipped topping, thawed, for garnish	2 cups	500 mL
Peach slices, for garnish		

Mix sugar and cornstarch in large saucepan. Stir in water, corn syrup and lemon juice. Heat and stir until boiling. Simmer for about 3 minutes. Remove from heat.

Stir in jelly powder until dissolved. To hasten cooling, set saucepan in cold water in sink. Stir often.

Add peaches to cooled mixture. Stir to coat. Pour into pie shell. Chill for at least 3 hours.

Garnish with whipped topping and peach slices. Cuts into 8 wedges.

1 wedge: 278 Calories; 7.6 g Total Fat; 172 mg Sodium; 3 g Protein; 52 g Carbohydrate; 1 g Dietary Fiber

Pictured on front cover.

Prep Time: 15 minutes to prepare and bake pie shell; 20 minutes to prepare filling.

To Make Ahead: Assemble and chill for up to 1 day. To serve, garnish as above. Do not freeze.

Paré Pointer

The mother ghost told the baby ghost to spook only when spooken to.

Danish Quiche

Piquant blue cheese flavor in this custard-like quiche.

Large eggs	3	3
All-purpose flour	1 tbsp.	15 mL
Grated Edam cheese	1 cup	250 mL
Danish blue cheese, crumbled and lightly packed	¼ cup	60 mL
Can of skim evaporated milk	13½ oz.	385 mL
Milk	¼ cup	60 mL
Salt	½ tsp.	2 mL
Pepper	⅛ tsp.	0.5 mL
Hot pepper sauce	⅛ tsp.	0.5 mL
Unbaked 9 inch (22 cm) pie shell	1	1
Green onions, finely chopped	2	2

Combine first 9 ingredients in blender. Process until smooth.

Pour egg mixture into pie shell. Sprinkle with green onion. Bake on bottom shelf in 350°F (175°C) oven for about 50 minutes. A knife inserted near center should come out clean. Let stand for 10 minutes before cutting. Serves 6.

1 serving: 343 Calories; 20 g Total Fat; 800 mg Sodium; 17 g Protein; 23 g Carbohydrate; trace Dietary Fiber

Prep Time: 10 minutes to prepare pie shell; 20 minutes to prepare filling.

To Make Ahead: Prepare blender contents. Prepare pie shell with onion in bottom. Cover and chill separately. To serve, assemble just before baking as above. Or bake, cool and cover early in day or night before. Reheat.

To Freeze: Bake, cool and cover in foil. Label. Freeze for up to 2 months. To serve, bring to room temperature, cover and heat in 325°F (160°C) oven until hot.

 When an egg is stuck to the carton, an easy way to ensure the egg won't break is to wet the carton where the egg is stuck and the egg should come right out without cracking.

Dilly Quiche

Good cheese and bacon flavor with a dash of dill.

Bacon slices, cooked crisp and crumbled	6	6
Grated light medium Cheddar cheese	1/2 cup	125 mL
Unbaked 9 inch (22 cm) pie shell	1	1
Large eggs	3	3
Skim evaporated milk	1 cup	250 mL
Light creamed cottage cheese	1 cup	250 mL
All-purpose flour	1 tbsp.	15 mL
Dry mustard	1/2 tsp.	2 mL
Dill weed	1/2 tsp.	2 mL
Onion powder	1/4 tsp.	1 mL
Salt	1/4 tsp.	1 mL
Pepper	1/16 tsp.	0.5 mL
Grated light Parmesan cheese	2 tbsp.	30 mL

Sprinkle bacon and Cheddar cheese in pie shell.

Combine next 9 ingredients in blender. Process until smooth. Pour over bacon and cheese. Bake on bottom shelf in 375°F (190°C) oven for about 30 minutes.

Sprinkle with Parmesan cheese. Bake for 10 minutes. A knife inserted near center should come out clean. Let stand for 10 minutes before cutting. Serves 6.

1 serving: 332 Calories; 18.6 g Total Fat; 749 mg Sodium; 19 g Protein; 21 g Carbohydrate; trace Dietary Fiber

Prep Time: 10 minutes to prepare pie shell; 20 minutes to prepare filling.

To Make Ahead: Prepare pie shell with bacon and cheese in bottom. Prepare blender contents. Cover and chill separately. To serve, assemble just before baking as above. Or bake, cool, cover and chill early in day or night before. Reheat.

To Freeze: Bake, cool and cover in foil. Label. Freeze for up to 2 months. To serve, bring to room temperature, cover and heat in 325°F (160°C) oven until hot.

Chicken Quiche

A full-meal deal with lots of flavor.

Cooking oil	1 tbsp.	15 mL
Boneless, skinless chicken breast halves (about 2), diced	½ lb.	225 g
Medium onion, chopped	1	1
Cauliflower florets	1½ cups	375 mL
Water	¼ cup	60 mL
Grated light sharp Cheddar cheese	½ cup	125 mL
Unbaked 9 inch (22 cm) pie shell	1	1
Large eggs	3	3
All-purpose flour	1 tbsp.	15 mL
Skim evaporated milk	⅔ cup	150 mL
Ground nutmeg, just a pinch		
Salt	¾ tsp.	4 mL
Pepper	¼ tsp.	1 mL
Green onions, chopped	2	2

Heat cooking oil in frying pan. Add chicken and onion. Sauté until golden.

Add cauliflower and water. Cover. Steam for 4 minutes until cauliflower is tender-crisp. Remove cover. Stir until water has evaporated. Cool.

Sprinkle cheese in bottom of pie shell. Spoon chicken mixture over top.

Beat eggs and flour in medium bowl until smooth. Beat in evaporated milk, nutmeg, salt and pepper. Pour over chicken.

Sprinkle with green onion. Bake on bottom shelf in 350°F (175°C) oven for 40 minutes. A knife inserted near center should come out clean. Let stand for 10 minutes before cutting. Serves 6.

1 serving: 322 Calories; 17.5 g Total Fat; 682 mg Sodium; 19 g Protein; 21 g Carbohydrate; 1 g Dietary Fiber

Pictured on page 71 and back cover.

Prep Time: 10 minutes to prepare pie shell; 15 minutes to prepare filling.

To Make Ahead: Prepare pie shell with cheese and green onion in bottom. Prepare chicken mixture. Prepare egg mixture. Cover and chill each separately. To serve, assemble just before baking as above. Or bake, cool, cover and chill early in day or night before. Reheat.

To Freeze: Bake, cool, cover and chill. Label. Freeze for up to 2 months. To serve, bring to room temperature, cover and heat in 325°F (160°C) oven until hot.

Asparagus Crab Quiche

Subtle crab flavor with background tastes of cheese, onion and asparagus.

Can of asparagus spears, drained	12 oz.	341 mL
Unbaked 9 inch (22 cm) pie shell	1	1
Cans of crabmeat (4¼ oz., 120 g, each), drained, cartilage removed	2	2
Large hard-boiled eggs, chopped	3	3
Finely diced celery	⅓ cup	75 mL
Finely chopped green onion	¼ cup	60 mL
Grated light sharp Cheddar cheese	1 cup	250 mL
Large eggs, fork-beaten	2	2
Milk	¼ cup	60 mL
Light mayonnaise (not salad dressing)	¾ cup	175 mL

Layer ½ of asparagus in bottom of pie shell.

Combine crabmeat, chopped egg, celery, green onion and cheese in bowl. Stir.

Beat remaining eggs in small bowl. Add milk and mayonnaise. Blend well. Stir egg mixture into crabmeat mixture. Pour over asparagus. Arrange remaining ½ of asparagus on top in spoke design. Bake on bottom shelf in 375°F (190°C) oven for 30 minutes. Reduce heat to 325°F (160°C). Bake for about 45 minutes. A knife inserted near center should come out clean. Let stand for 10 minutes before cutting. Serves 6.

1 serving: 387 Calories; 26.9 g Total Fat; 1040 mg Sodium; 17 g Protein; 19 g Carbohydrate; 1 g Dietary Fiber

Pictured on page 108.

Prep Time: 10 minutes to prepare pie shell; 20 minutes to prepare filling.

To Make Ahead: Prepare pie shell and filling early in day or night before. Cover and chill separately. To serve, assemble just before baking as above. Bake, cool, cover and chill early in the day or night before.

To Freeze: Bake, cool and cover in foil. Label. Freeze for up to 2 months. To serve, bring to room temperature, cover and heat in 325°F (160°C) oven until hot.

Chicken Strata

The smell of this cooking will make everyone very hungry!

Boneless, skinless chicken breast halves (about 6), cut into ¾ inch (2 cm) cubes	1½ lbs.	680 g
Cooking oil	1 tbsp.	15 mL
Sliced fresh mushrooms	2 cups	500 mL
Whole wheat (or white) bread slices, crusts removed, cubed (about 4 cups, 1 L, packed)	8	8
Large eggs	4	4
Milk	1 cup	250 mL
Can of condensed cream of chicken (or mushroom) soup	10 oz.	284 mL
Light salad dressing (or mayonnaise)	⅓ cup	75 mL
Jar of sliced pimiento, drained and diced	2 oz.	57 mL
Dry mustard	½ tsp.	2 mL
Parsley flakes	2 tsp.	10 mL
Onion powder	¼ tsp.	1 mL
Grated light sharp Cheddar cheese	¾ cup	175 mL
Salt	¼ tsp.	1 mL
Pepper, sprinkle		
Margarine (or butter)	2 tbsp.	30 mL
Dry bread crumbs	½ cup	125 mL

Sauté chicken in cooking oil in frying pan until browned and no pink remains. Transfer to medium bowl.

Add mushrooms to frying pan. Sauté until golden. Add to chicken. Stir.

Place bread cubes in well-greased 3 quart (3 L) casserole.

Beat eggs in large bowl until smooth. Beat in milk, soup and salad dressing. Stir in pimiento, mustard, parsley, onion powder, cheese, salt and pepper. Pour ½ of milk mixture over bread cubes. Spoon chicken mixture over top. Pour remaining ½ of milk mixture over all. Cover. Chill overnight.

(continued on next page)

Eggs

Melt margarine in small saucepan. Stir in bread crumbs. Sprinkle over casserole. Bake, uncovered, in 350°F (175°C) oven for about 1¼ hours. A knife inserted in center should come out clean. Let stand for 10 minutes. Serves 6.

1 serving: 508 Calories; 22.4 g Total Fat; 1144 mg Sodium; 42 g Protein; 34 g Carbohydrate; 3 g Dietary Fiber

Prep Time: 20 minutes to prepare and assemble; overnight to chill.

To Make Ahead: Must be assembled early in day or night before. Cover. Chill. To serve, bake as above. Do not freeze.

Reuben Strata

You'll love the traditional corned beef flavor that comes through. Serve at your next watch-sports-on-TV party.

Whole wheat (or white) bread slices, crusts removed	12	12
Can of corned beef, crumbled	12 oz.	340 g
Can of sauerkraut, drained and rinsed	14 oz.	398 mL
Grated light Swiss (or Cheddar) cheese	1 cup	250 mL
Large eggs	5	5
Milk	2 cups	500 mL
Minced onion flakes	2 tbsp.	30 mL
Worcestershire sauce	1 tsp.	5 mL
Salt	¼ tsp.	1 mL
Pepper	⅛ tsp.	0.5 mL

Cover bottom of well-greased 9 x 13 inch (22 x 33 cm) pan with 6 bread slices. Sprinkle corned beef over bread. Spoon sauerkraut over corned beef. Scatter cheese over sauerkraut. Cover with remaining 6 bread slices.

Beat eggs in medium bowl until smooth. Add milk, onion flakes, Worcestershire sauce, salt and pepper. Beat to mix. Pour over all. Cover. Chill overnight. Bake, uncovered, in 350°F (175°C) oven for 1¼ to 1½ hours. A knife inserted in center should come out clean. Let stand for 10 minutes. Serves 6.

1 serving: 439 Calories; 18.9 g Total Fat; 1415 mg Sodium; 34 g Protein; 34 g Carbohydrate; 4 g Dietary Fiber

Prep Time: 20 minutes to prepare and assemble; overnight to chill.

To Make Ahead: Must be assembled early in day or night before. Cover. Chill. To serve, bake as above. Do not freeze.

Cheese Strata

Cheesy with a crispy topping. Excellent choice for a brunch or lunch.

Whole wheat (or white) bread slices, crusts removed	12	12
Light sharp Cheddar cheese, sliced	8 oz.	225 g
Sliced green onion (optional)	⅓ cup	75 mL
Salt	1 tsp.	5 mL
Dry mustard	1 tsp.	5 mL
Onion powder	¼ tsp.	1 mL
Large eggs	6	6
Milk	3 cups	750 mL
Crisp rice cereal, crushed	1 cup	250 mL

Cover bottom of well-greased 9 x 13 inch (22 x 33 cm) pan with 6 bread slices. Lay cheese slices over top to cover. Sprinkle with green onion. Cover cheese with remaining 6 bread slices.

Mix salt, mustard and onion powder in small cup. Sprinkle over top.

Beat eggs in large bowl until smooth. Add milk. Beat to mix. Pour over all.

Sprinkle with crushed cereal. Cover. Chill overnight. Bake, uncovered, in 350°F (175°C) oven for about 1 hour. A knife inserted in center should come out clean. Let stand for 10 minutes. Serves 6.

1 serving: 385 Calories; 15.4 g Total Fat; 1139 mg Sodium; 25 g Protein; 37 g Carbohydrate; 3 g Dietary Fiber

Pictured on page 107.

Prep Time: 20 minutes to prepare and assemble; overnight to chill.

To Make Ahead: Must be assembled early in day or night before. Cover. Chill. To serve, bake as above. Do not freeze.

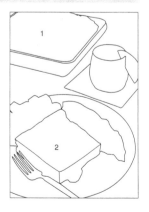

1. Apple Coffee Cake, page 62
2. Cheese Strata, above

Props Courtesy Of: Chintz & Company
                     Stokes

Baked Breakfast

Consistency of bread pudding but with a mild cheese flavor.

Whole wheat (or white) bread slices, with crusts, cut into 1 inch (2.5 cm) cubes	4	4
Grated light sharp Cheddar cheese	1 cup	250 mL
Large eggs	2	2
Milk	2 cups	500 mL
Salt	¼ tsp.	1 mL
Pepper	¹⁄₁₆ tsp.	0.5 mL

Arrange bread cubes in greased 2 quart (2 L) casserole. Sprinkle cheese over top.

Beat eggs in medium bowl until smooth. Beat in milk, salt and pepper. Pour evenly over bread and cheese. Chill overnight. Bake in 350°F (175°C) oven for about 40 minutes until golden. A knife inserted in center should come out clean. Let stand for 10 minutes. Serves 4.

1 serving: 250 Calories; 10.6 g Total Fat; 605 mg Sodium; 17 g Protein; 21 g Carbohydrate; 2 g Dietary Fiber

Prep Time: 15 minutes to prepare and assemble; chill overnight.

To Make Ahead: Must be assembled early in day or night before. Cover. Chill. To serve, bake as above. Do not freeze.

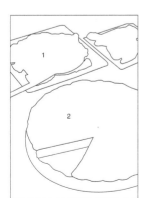

1. Roasted Pepper Salad, page 129
2. Asparagus Crab Quiche, page 103

Props Courtesy Of: Chintz & Company

Seafood Supreme

You have the option of a more full-bodied dish, by doubling the crabmeat and shrimp. Omit topping if serving in patty shells or over pasta.

Margarine (or butter)	2 tbsp.	30 mL
Frozen scallops, thawed and drained (or fresh), halved or quartered if large	8 oz.	225 g
Can of crabmeat, drained, cartilage removed	4¹/₅ oz.	120 g
Can of shrimp, drained and rinsed	4 oz.	113 g
All-purpose flour	¼ cup	60 mL
Salt	½ tsp.	2 mL
Pepper	⅛ tsp.	0.5 mL
Paprika	⅛ tsp.	0.5 mL
Milk	1½ cups	375 mL
Sherry (or alcohol-free sherry)	2 tbsp.	30 mL
TOPPING		
Margarine (or butter)	2 tbsp.	30 mL
Dry bread crumbs	½ cup	125 mL
Grated light sharp Cheddar cheese	¼ cup	60 mL

Heat margarine in frying pan. Add scallops. Stir-fry for 3 to 4 minutes until opaque.

Stir in crabmeat and shrimp. Sprinkle with flour, salt, pepper and paprika. Mix. Stir in milk and sherry until mixture is boiling and thickened. Turn into ungreased 1½ quart (1.5 L) casserole.

Topping: Melt margarine in small saucepan. Stir in bread crumbs and cheese. Sprinkle over seafood mixture. Cover. Bake in 350°F (175°C) oven for 30 to 35 minutes until hot and browned. Serves 6.

1 serving: 240 Calories; 10.8 g Total Fat; 671 mg Sodium; 18 g Protein; 16 g Carbohydrate; trace Dietary Fiber

Pictured on page 125.

Prep Time: 15 minutes to prepare and assemble.

To Make Ahead: Assemble early in day or night before. Cover. Chill. To serve, bake as above.

To Freeze: Bake, cool and cover casserole. Label. Freeze for up to 2 months. To serve, thaw and heat as above for 15 minutes until hot. To heat from baked frozen state, see Tip, page 69.

Shrimp Istanbul

Serve over your favorite pasta or rice. Slightly sweet with a tang from sour cream.

Raw shelled shrimp	1 lb.	454 g
Margarine (or butter)	1 tbsp.	15 mL
Margarine (or butter)	1 tbsp.	15 mL
Sliced fresh mushrooms	1 cup	250 mL
Small onions, thinly sliced	2	2
Can of skim evaporated milk, 2 tbsp. (30 mL) reserved	13½ oz.	385 mL
Tomato sauce	3 tbsp.	50 mL
Sherry (or alcohol-free sherry)	2 tbsp.	30 mL
Reserved skim evaporated milk	2 tbsp.	30 mL
Cornstarch	2½ tbsp.	37 mL
Light sour cream	½ cup	125 mL

Sauté shrimp and first amount of margarine in frying pan for about 5 minutes. Transfer shrimp to bowl.

Add second amount of margarine to frying pan. Add mushrooms and onion. Sauté for about 5 minutes until tender.

Slowly stir in first amount of evaporated milk, tomato sauce and sherry. Add shrimp. Simmer 2 minutes.

Mix reserved evaporated milk into cornstarch in small cup. Stir into shrimp mixture until boiling and thickened.

Gently stir in sour cream. Pour into 2 quart (2 L) casserole. Cover. Bake in 350°F (175°C) oven for 30 to 35 minutes until hot. Makes 6 cups (1.5 L). Serves 6.

1 serving: 217 Calories; 6.9 g Total Fat; 295 mg Sodium; 22 g Protein; 16 g Carbohydrate; 1 g Dietary Fiber

Prep Time: 10 minutes to prepare and assemble.

To Make Ahead: Assemble early in day or night before. Cover. Chill. To serve, bake as above.

To Freeze: Use fresh shrimp if freezing. Cover unbaked casserole. Label. Freeze for up to 2 months. To serve, thaw and bake as above. To bake from frozen state, see Tip, page 69.

Shrimp Elegant

Your guests will never know you opened a can for the
creamy base! Rich flavor. Serve over rice or noodles.

Cooking oil	2 tsp.	10 mL
Medium onion, chopped	1	1
Sliced fresh mushrooms	3 cups	750 mL
Can of condensed cream of mushroom soup	10 oz.	284 mL
Light salad dressing (or mayonnaise)	¼ cup	60 mL
Lemon juice	2 tsp.	10 mL
Salt	½ tsp.	2 mL
Lemon pepper	¾ tsp.	4 mL
Garlic powder	¼ tsp.	1 mL
Medium cooked shrimp (3 cups, 750 mL)	15 oz.	425 g
Light sour cream	½ cup	125 mL
Chopped fresh parsley	2 tbsp.	30 mL

Heat cooking oil in large non-stick frying pan. Add onion. Sauté until soft. Transfer to bowl.

Add mushrooms to frying pan. Sauté until golden. Add cooked onion.

Mix next 6 ingredients in small bowl. Pour over onion and mushrooms. Heat until bubbling.

Stir in shrimp. Heat until shrimp is hot. Add sour cream and parsley, stirring continually, until hot. Do not boil. Makes 5 cups (1.25 L). Serves 6.

1 serving: 206 Calories; 10.4 g Total Fat; 893 mg Sodium; 18 g Protein; 10 g Carbohydrate; 1 g Dietary Fiber

Prep Time: 10 minutes to prepare and assemble.

To Make Ahead: Prepare early in day or night before. Cover. Chill. To serve, reheat without boiling. Do not freeze as the cream of mushroom soup, salad dressing and sour cream may separate.

Paré Pointer
Ghosts take coffin drops for colds.

Halibut Casserole

The green beans stay tender-crisp in this mild casserole. The fish is tender and flaky.

Fresh halibut fillets or other firm fleshed fish (or use frozen, thawed and blotted dry), cut bite size	1½ lbs.	680 g
Frozen cut green beans	2 cups	500 mL
Cooking oil	1 tbsp.	15 mL
Chopped onion	¾ cup	175 mL
All-purpose flour	3 tbsp.	50 mL
Milk	2 cups	500 mL
Dill weed	1 tsp.	5 mL
Salt	¾ tsp.	4 mL
Pepper	½ tsp.	2 mL
Margarine (or butter)	2 tbsp.	30 mL
Dry bread crumbs	½ cup	125 mL
Poultry seasoning	¼ tsp.	1 mL
Onion powder	¼ tsp.	1 mL
Salt	1/16 tsp.	0.5 mL
Pepper, just a pinch		

Place fish pieces in ungreased 3 quart (3 L) casserole. Scatter beans over top.

Heat cooking oil in medium frying pan. Add onion. Sauté until soft.

Quickly mix flour into onion. Stir in milk until mixture is boiling and thickened. Add dill weed and first amounts of salt and pepper. Stir. Makes 2 cups (500 mL) sauce. Pour over fish and beans.

Melt margarine in small saucepan. Stir in remaining 5 ingredients. Sprinkle over all. Bake, uncovered, in 400°F (205°C) oven for 40 minutes. Serves 6.

1 serving: 290 Calories; 10.3 g Total Fat; 594 mg Sodium; 29 g Protein; 19 g Carbohydrate; 2 g Dietary Fiber

Prep Time: 20 minutes to prepare and assemble.

To Make Ahead: Assemble early in day or night before. Cover. Chill. To serve, bake as above.

To Freeze: Bake, cool and cover casserole with foil. Label. Freeze for up to 2 months. To serve, thaw and heat as above until hot. To bake from frozen state, see Tip, page 69.

Single Quick Macaroni

A quick economical snack or meal anytime. Use microwave for cooking.

Elbow macaroni, uncooked	2 cups	500 mL
Powdered Cheddar cheese product	½ cup	125 mL
Skim milk powder	½ cup	125 mL
Salt	½ tsp.	2 mL

Place ½ cup (125 mL) macaroni in four small sealable plastic freezer bags.

Process cheese product, skim milk powder and salt in blender until smooth. Place about ¼ cup (60 mL) in another 4 small sealable plastic freezer bags. Clip 1 of each bag together. Attach the following directions:

Directions: Put macaroni from 1 packet and 1¼ cups (300 mL) water in 2 cup (500 mL) bowl. Microwave, uncovered, on high (100%) for 9 minutes until tender but firm. Do not drain.

Add 1 packet of cheese mixture. Stir well. Let stand for 2 minutes to thicken. Makes 1 cup (250 mL) per packet set, enough for 1 serving.

1 serving: 609 Calories; 14.4 g Total Fat; 2546 mg Sodium; 40 g Protein; 78 g Carbohydrate; 1 g Dietary Fiber

Prep Time: 10 minutes to assemble packets; 12 minutes to prepare 1 packet.

To Make Ahead: Assemble, label and store in cupboard for up to 2 months.

Macaroni Bake

Notable cheese and mushroom flavor.

Elbow macaroni, uncooked	2 cups	500 mL
Can of condensed cream of mushroom soup	10 oz.	284 mL
Can of mushroom pieces, drained	10 oz.	284 mL
Milk	2½ cups	625 mL
Grated light sharp Cheddar cheese	1 cup	250 mL
Grated Parmesan cheese	⅓ cup	75 mL
Salt	½ tsp.	2 mL
Pepper	⅛ tsp.	0.5 mL

(continued on next page)

Pour macaroni into ungreased 2 quart (2 L) casserole.

Mix remaining 7 ingredients in medium bowl. Pour over macaroni. Stir. Push any visible macaroni underneath surface. Cover. Bake in 350°F (175°C) oven for about 60 minutes until macaroni is tender. Serves 4.

1 serving: 490 Calories; 17 g Total Fat; 1538 mg Sodium; 25 g Protein; 57 g Carbohydrate; 3 g Dietary Fiber

---

Prep Time: 20 minutes to prepare and assemble.

To Make Ahead: Assemble early in day or night before. Cover. Chill. To serve, bake as above.

Creamy Noodles

Nice dill flavor in plenty of creamy sauce.

Broad noodles	3 cups	750 mL
Boiling water	2½ qts.	2.5 L
Cooking oil (optional)	1 tbsp.	15 mL
Salt	2 tsp.	10 mL
Milk	2 cups	500 mL
All-purpose flour	¼ cup	60 mL
Salt	¾ tsp.	4 mL
Pepper	⅛ tsp.	0.5 mL
Dill weed	¼ tsp.	1 mL
Margarine (or butter)	1 tbsp.	15 mL

Cook noodles in boiling water, cooking oil and salt in large uncovered pot or Dutch oven for 5 to 7 minutes until tender but firm. Drain. Return to pot.

Gradually stir milk into flour in medium saucepan until no lumps remain. Add salt, pepper, dill weed and margarine. Heat and stir until boiling and thickened. Remove from heat. Stir into noodles. Makes 4 cups (1 L).

1 cup (250 mL): 226 Calories; 5.7 g Total Fat; 614 mg Sodium; 9 g Protein; 34 g Carbohydrate; 1 g Dietary Fiber

---

Prep Time: 10 minutes to prepare and assemble.

To Make Ahead: Make early in day or night before. Cover. Chill. To serve, turn into greased 1½ quart (1.5 L) casserole. Cover. Heat in 350°F (175°C) oven for 30 minutes until hot.

To Freeze: Divide between two 2½ cup (625 mL) freezer containers (or size of choice). Label. Freeze for up to 2 months. To serve, thaw and bake as above. May need to add 1 tbsp. (15 mL) water or milk to restore creamy texture.

Select-A-Meal: See page 12.

Curried Pasta

Mild curry flavor. Chutney adds a subtle "something."

Large shell pasta (not jumbo)	4$\frac{1}{2}$ cups	1.1 L
Boiling water	3 qts.	3 L
Cooking oil (optional)	1 tbsp.	15 mL
Salt	1 tbsp.	15 mL
Milk	2$\frac{1}{4}$ cups	560 mL
All-purpose flour	$\frac{1}{4}$ cup	60 mL
Curry powder	1$\frac{1}{2}$ tsp.	7 mL
Parsley flakes	1 tsp.	5 mL
Chicken bouillon powder	1 tsp.	5 mL
Salt	$\frac{1}{2}$ tsp.	2 mL
Pepper	$\frac{1}{4}$ tsp.	1 mL
Mango (or other) chutney	1 tbsp.	15 mL

Cook pasta in boiling water, cooking oil and salt in large uncovered pot or Dutch oven for 13 to 16 minutes until tender but firm. Drain. Return pasta to pot.

Gradually stir milk into flour in medium saucepan until no lumps remain. Add curry powder, parsley, bouillon powder, salt and pepper. Heat and stir until boiling and thickened. Remove from heat.

Stir in chutney. Add sauce to pasta. Stir. Makes 6 cups (1.5 L).

1 cup (250 mL): 314 Calories; 2.3 g Total Fat; 388 mg Sodium; 12 g Protein; 60 g Carbohydrate; 2 g Dietary Fiber

Prep Time: 10 minutes to prepare sauce while pasta cooks.

To Make Ahead: Make early in day or night before. Cool. To serve, turn into greased 1$\frac{1}{2}$ quart (1.5 L) casserole. Cover. Heat in 350°F (175°C) oven for 30 minutes until hot.

To Freeze: Divide among three 2$\frac{1}{2}$ cup (625 mL) freezer containers (or size of choice). Label. Freeze for up to 2 months. To serve, thaw and bake as above. May need to add 1 tbsp. (15 mL) water or milk to restore creamy texture.

Select-A-Meal: See page 12.

Paré Pointer

He decided to follow the medical profession so he became an undertaker.

Ham Loaves

Attractive individual servings in a mini meatloaf with a sweet mustardy glaze.
Double or triple the glaze to serve as a sauce over ham loaves.

Large egg, fork-beaten	1	1
Light salad dressing (or mayonnaise)	2 tbsp.	30 mL
Light sour cream	2 tbsp.	30 mL
Sweet pickle relish	2 tbsp.	30 mL
Grated light Parmesan cheese	2 tbsp.	30 mL
Dry mustard	1/4 tsp.	1 mL
Fine dry bread crumbs	2/3 cup	150 mL
Ground cooked ham (about 2 1/4 cups, 560 mL)	1 lb.	454 g
GLAZE		
Brown sugar, packed	1/3 cup	75 mL
Prepared mustard	2 tsp.	10 mL
Prepared orange juice	1 1/2 tsp.	7 mL

Mix first 7 ingredients well in medium bowl.

Add ham. Mix. Divide into 4 equal portions. Shape each portion into small meatloaf. Arrange on greased baking sheet.

Glaze: Stir brown sugar, mustard and orange juice in small saucepan. Heat on medium until sugar is dissolved. Brush sauce over loaves. Bake in 350°F (175°C) oven for about 35 minutes. Makes 4 mini loaves.

1 mini loaf: 335 Calories; 10.1 g Total Fat; 1787 mg Sodium; 28 g Protein; 32 g Carbohydrate; 1 g Dietary Fiber

Pictured on page 143.

Prep Time: 20 minutes includes grinding ham.

To Make Ahead: Assemble early in day or night before. Cover. Chill loaves and sauce separately. To serve, heat sauce and bake as above.

To Freeze: Wrap unbaked individual loaves without glaze. Label. Freeze for up to 2 months. To serve, thaw and bake wrapped loaves as above. Serve loaves brushed with glaze.

Select-A-Meal: See page 12.

Pizza Casserole

Real cheesy pizza flavor in a hearty casserole.

Pepperoni slices, cut into ¼ inch (6 mm) pieces (about 4-5 small sticks)	1½ cups	375 mL
Water	1½ cups	375 mL
Margarine (or butter)	2 tsp.	10 mL
Medium onion, chopped	1	1
Cans of tomato sauce (7½ oz., 213 mL, each)	2	2
Can of mushroom pieces, drained	10 oz.	284 mL
Dried whole oregano	1 tsp.	5 mL
Dried sweet basil	1 tsp.	5 mL
Tiny shell pasta	2 cups	500 mL
Boiling water	2½ qts.	2.5 L
Cooking oil (optional)	1 tbsp.	15 mL
Salt	2 tsp.	10 mL
Grated light Parmesan cheese	3 tbsp.	50 mL
Grated part-skim mozzarella cheese	1 cup	250 mL
Grated part-skim mozzarella cheese	2 cups	500 mL

Combine pepperoni with first amount of water in medium saucepan. Bring to a boil. Simmer for 4 to 5 minutes. Drain.

Melt margarine in frying pan. Add onion. Sauté until soft. Add tomato sauce, mushrooms, oregano and basil. Stir. Remove from heat.

Cook pasta in boiling water, cooking oil and salt in large uncovered pot or Dutch oven for 8 to 10 minutes until tender but firm. Drain. Turn into 3 quart (3 L) casserole.

Add Parmesan cheese. Toss well.

Sprinkle with first amount of mozzarella cheese. Scatter pepperoni slices over top. Cover with tomato-onion sauce.

Sprinkle remaining mozzarella cheese over all. Bake, uncovered, in 350°F (175°C) oven for about 30 minutes until bubbly and lightly browned. Serves 6.

1 serving: 518 Calories; 28.6 g Total Fat; 1658 mg Sodium; 30 g Protein; 36 g Carbohydrate; 3 g Dietary Fiber

Prep Time: 30 minutes to prepare and assemble.

To Make Ahead: Assemble early in day or night before. Cover. Chill. To serve, bake as above.

To Freeze: Cover unbaked casserole. Label. Freeze for up to 2 months. To serve, thaw and bake as above. To bake from frozen state, see Tip, page 69.

Ham Florentine Bake

Lots of creamy sauce. What a superb way to eat your spinach!

Black Forest ham steaks (4 small) or 1 large steak, cut into 4 portions	1 lb.	454 g
Frozen chopped spinach, thawed and squeezed dry	10 oz.	300 g
SAUCE		
Milk	1½ cups	375 mL
All-purpose flour	3 tbsp.	50 mL
Prepared mustard	1 tsp.	5 mL
Dried whole oregano	¼ tsp.	1 mL
Ground nutmeg	1/16 tsp.	0.5 mL
Pepper	⅛ tsp.	0.5 mL
Grated light sharp Cheddar cheese	1 cup	250 mL

Arrange ham steaks in shallow greased 2 quart (2 L) casserole. Cover each steak with spinach.

Sauce: Whisk milk gradually into flour in medium saucepan until smooth. Add mustard, oregano, nutmeg and pepper. Stir in cheese. Heat and stir until boiling and thickened. Pour sauce over spinach. Bake, uncovered, in 350°F (175°C) oven for 30 minutes until spinach is tender and ham is hot. Serves 4.

1 serving: 303 Calories; 12.1 g Total Fat; 1729 mg Sodium; 35 g Protein; 12 g Carbohydrate; 2 g Dietary Fiber

Prep Time: 10 minutes to prepare and assemble.

To Make Ahead: Assemble completely or prepare sauce only early in day or night before. Cover. Chill. To serve, bake as above. Do not freeze.

Gang's All Here Meal

Thick chili-like dish. A tangy tomato flavor with a touch of sweetness. Wonderful flavor.

Sausage meat	2 lbs.	900 g
Cans of beans in tomato sauce (14 oz., 398 mL, each)	2	2
Cans of red kidney beans (14 oz., 398 mL, each), with liquid	2	2
Can of chick peas (garbanzo beans), drained	19 oz.	540 mL
Can of cut green beans, drained	14 oz.	398 mL
Can of cut wax beans, drained	14 oz.	398 mL
Medium onion, chopped	1	1
Brown sugar, packed	1 cup	250 mL
Can of tomato paste	5½ oz.	156 mL
Ketchup	¾ cup	175 mL

Scramble-fry sausage meat in frying pan until browned. Drain. Transfer meat to ungreased 4 quart (4 L) casserole or small roaster.

Add remaining 9 ingredients. Stir well. Cover. Bake in 275°F (140°C) oven for 4 hours. Makes 13 cups (3.25 L). Serves 6.

1 serving: 817 Calories; 28.1 g Total Fat; 2330 mg Sodium; 30 g Protein; 120 g Carbohydrate; 25 g Dietary Fiber

Pictured on front cover.

Prep Time: 15 minutes to brown and drain sausage; 20 minutes to assemble rest of casserole.

To Make Ahead: Assemble early in day or night before. Cover. Chill. To serve, bake as above.

To Freeze: Cover unbaked casserole. Label. Freeze for up to 2 months. To serve, thaw and bake as above. To heat from frozen state, see Tip, page 69.

 Freeze casserole in its dish, then remove frozen contents and wrap in foil so casserole dish is available for use. When ready to use, pop the frozen block into same casserole dish. See Tip, page 69.

Stuffed Tomato Salad

Fresh vegetables and ham make this a refreshing but filling salad.

Large tomatoes	6	6
Orzo (small bow pasta)	1 cup	250 mL
Boiling water	6 cups	1.5 L
Salt	1 tsp.	5 mL
Light salad dressing (or mayonnaise)	¼ cup	60 mL
Prepared mustard	2 tsp.	10 mL
Grated red onion	2 tbsp.	30 mL
Dill weed	¼ tsp.	1 mL
Pepper, sprinkle		
Can of ham flakes, drained and broken up	6½ oz.	184 g
Diced celery	½ cup	125 mL
Diced green pepper	¼ cup	60 mL
Jar of chopped pimiento, drained	2 oz.	57 mL
Green onions, chopped	2	2

Cut off slice from stem end of each tomato. Using teaspoon, scoop out pulp and seeds leaving shell about ¼ inch (6 mm) thick. Turn upside down to drain.

Cook pasta in boiling water and salt in large uncovered saucepan. Drain. Rinse in cold water. Drain well.

Mix next 5 ingredients in medium bowl. Add cooked pasta.

Add ham, celery, green pepper, pimiento and green onion. Stir. Divide filling among tomatoes. Makes 6 stuffed tomatoes. Do not freeze.

1 stuffed tomato: 299 Calories; 9.8 g Total Fat; 552 mg Sodium; 12 g Protein; 42 g Carbohydrate; 3 g Dietary Fiber

Pictured on page 89.

Variation: Substitute tuna for ham flakes.

Prep Time: 15 minutes to prepare filling while pasta cooks.

To Make Ahead: Prepare tomatoes and filling night before. Cover and chill tomatoes and filling separately. To serve, stuff tomatoes. Do not freeze.

Oriental Bean Salad

Well worth making. Keeps in the refrigerator for up to two weeks.

Can of Oriental vegetables, drained	19 oz.	540 mL
Can of cut green beans, drained	14 oz.	398 mL
Can of cut wax beans, drained	14 oz.	398 mL
Medium onion, thinly sliced	1	1
Small green pepper, cut up	1	1
Sliced celery	2 cups	500 mL
Can of sliced water chestnuts, drained	8 oz.	227 mL
Granulated sugar	1½ cups	375 mL
White vinegar	¾ cup	175 mL
Cooking oil	¾ cup	175 mL
Salt	½ tsp.	2 mL

Rinse Oriental vegetables. Drain well. Put into large bowl. Add next 6 ingredients. Stir.

Measure remaining 4 ingredients into medium saucepan. Heat, stirring occasionally, until boiling. Pour over vegetables, pressing down with spoon. Cover. Chill for 24 hours, stirring occasionally. Remove with slotted spoon to serve. Keep unused salad chilled in brine. Makes 8 cups (2 L).

1 cup (250 mL): 413 Calories; 22 g Total Fat; 415 mg Sodium; 3 g Protein; 55 g Carbohydrate; 4 g Dietary Fiber

Pictured on page 17.

Prep Time: 15 minutes to prepare and assemble; 24 hours to chill.

To Make Ahead: Must be assembled for at least 24 hours before serving. Cover. Keeps in the refrigerator for up to two weeks.

Crispy Cukes

A sweet and sour flavor.

Granulated sugar	1 cup	250 mL
Water	1 cup	250 mL
White vinegar	1 cup	250 mL
Salt	1 tbsp.	15 mL
Pepper	¼ tsp.	1 mL
Onion powder	¼ tsp.	1 mL
Medium cucumbers, with peel	4	4

(continued on next page)

Mix first 6 ingredients well in large bowl. Stir until sugar is dissolved.

Draw fork down length of cucumbers all around, piercing peel. Thinly slice. Add to vinegar mixture. Stir. Cover. Chill for at least 24 hours. Makes 6½ cups (1.6 L).

½ cup (125 mL): 79 Calories; 0.1 g Total Fat; 539 mg Sodium; 1 g Protein; 20 g Carbohydrate; 1 g Dietary Fiber

Pictured on page 71 and back cover.

Prep Time: 5 minutes to prepare and assemble; 24 hours to chill.

To Make Ahead: Must be assembled at least 24 hours before serving. Keeps in the refrigerator for at least one week. Do not freeze.

Cheesy Green Salad

Add one cup (250 mL) crabmeat, shrimp or chicken if desired.

Cut or torn salad greens, 1 or more kinds, lightly packed	6 cups	1.5 L
Grated light sharp Cheddar (or crumbled goat) cheese	½ cup	125 mL
DRESSING		
Light salad dressing (or mayonnaise)	2 tbsp.	30 mL
Light sour cream	2 tbsp.	30 mL
Chopped fresh parsley	2 tbsp.	30 mL
Anchovy paste	½ tsp.	2 mL
Chopped green onion	2 tbsp.	30 mL
Garlic powder (or 1 clove, minced)	¼ tsp.	1 mL
Tarragon vinegar	2 tsp.	10 mL
Lemon juice	½ tsp.	2 mL

Combine torn greens and cheese in bowl.

Dressing: Mix all 8 ingredients in small bowl. Combine greens and cheese with dressing. Toss. Makes 6 cups (1.5 L).

1 cup (250 mL): 61 Calories; 3.8 g Total Fat; 141 mg Sodium; 4 g Protein; 3 g Carbohydrate; 1 g Dietary Fiber

Pictured on page 143.

Prep Time: 15 minutes to prepare and assemble.

To Make Ahead: Prepare early in day or night before. Cover and chill greens, cheese and dressing separately. To serve, assemble. Do not freeze.

Overnight Coleslaw

This will become a store-in-the-refrigerator favorite! A sweet slaw flavor.

Medium head of cabbage, shredded (about 2½ lbs., 1.1 kg)	1	1
Medium onion, thinly sliced	1	1
Green pepper, cut into short thin strips	1	1
White vinegar	1 cup	250 mL
Cooking oil	⅔ cup	150 mL
Granulated sugar	½ cup	125 mL
Prepared mustard	2 tsp.	10 mL
Celery seed	1 tsp.	5 mL
Salt	1 tsp.	5 mL
Pepper	¼ tsp.	1 mL

Combine cabbage, onion and green pepper in large container with lid.

Measure remaining 7 ingredients into medium saucepan. Heat on medium-high, stirring occasionally, until boiling. Boil for 30 seconds. Pour over vegetables. Press and stir to wilt vegetables so that brine covers well. Place lid on container. Chill for 24 hours. Makes about 10 cups (2.5 L).

½ cup (125 mL): 105 Calories; 7.8 g Total Fat; 152 mg Sodium; 1 g Protein; 9 g Carbohydrate; 1 g Dietary Fiber

Prep Time: 25 minutes to prepare and assemble; 24 hours to chill.

To Make Ahead: Must be assembled at least 24 hours before serving. Keeps in the refrigerator for at least one week. Do not freeze.

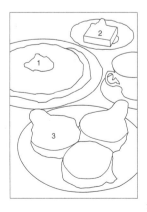

1. Party Salad, page 130
2. Gingerbread Cake, page 63
3. Seafood Supreme, page 110

Spinach Salad

Triple the dressing to have some on hand for any lettuce or mixed greens. It will keep for several weeks.

Bag of spinach, cut or torn	10 oz.	285 g
Fresh bean sprouts	1 cup	250 mL
Large hard-boiled eggs, chopped	2	2
Bacon slices, cooked crisp and crumbled	4	4
Thin short red onion slices	½ cup	125 mL
DRESSING		
White vinegar	3 tbsp.	50 mL
Granulated sugar	¼ cup	60 mL
Salt	¼ tsp.	1 mL
Cooking oil	1 tsp.	5 mL

Toss first 5 ingredients in bowl.

Dressing: Place remaining 4 ingredients in small bowl. Stir until sugar is dissolved. Pour dressing over salad. Toss. Serves 8.

1 serving: 85 Calories; 3.6 g Total Fat; 180 mg Sodium; 4 g Protein; 10 g Carbohydrate; 1 g Dietary Fiber

Pictured on front cover.

Prep Time: 15 to 20 minutes to prepare and assemble.

To Make Ahead: Prepare early in day. Cover and chill salad and dressing separately. To serve, assemble. Do not freeze.

1. Bread Stuffing, page 147
2. Mashed Potatoes Select, page 138
3. Pickled Beet Salad, page 131
4. Mushroom Sauce, page 31
5. Turkey Schnitzel, page 83

Props Courtesy Of: The Bay
                    X/S Wares

Twenty-Four Hour Salad

So many contrasts in texture make this salad an interesting accompaniment.

Granulated sugar	½ cup	125 mL
All-purpose flour	2 tsp.	10 mL
Reserved pineapple juice	⅔ cup	150 mL
White vinegar	2 tsp.	10 mL
Large egg	1	1
Can of pineapple tidbits, drained, juice reserved	14 oz.	398 mL
Miniature marshmallows	2 cups	500 mL
Seedless red grapes, halved	½ cup	125 mL
Envelope of dessert topping (not prepared)	1	1
Milk	½ cup	125 mL
Vanilla	½ tsp.	2 mL
Diced apple (about 1 large), with peel	1½ cups	375 mL
Chopped walnuts (or pecans)	½ cup	125 mL

Stir sugar and flour in medium saucepan. Add pineapple juice, vinegar and egg. Mix. Heat on medium, stirring constantly, until simmering and thickened. Do not overcook or it may curdle. Cool thoroughly.

Combine pineapple, marshmallows and grapes in medium bowl. Add egg mixture. Stir.

Beat dessert topping, milk and vanilla in small bowl until stiff. Fold in.

Add apple and walnuts. Fold in. Cover. Chill for 24 hours. Makes 7 cups (1.75 L). Serves 6.

1 serving: 321 Calories; 10.9 g Total Fat; 46 mg Sodium; 4 g Protein; 55 g Carbohydrate; 2 g Dietary Fiber

Prep Time: 15 minutes to prepare and assemble; 24 hours to chill.

To Make Ahead: Must be assembled at least 24 hours before serving. Cover. Keeps in the refrigerator for up to 2 days. Do not freeze.

Roasted Pepper Salad

A rainbow of colors with a mellowed pepper flavor.

Large green peppers	2	2
Large red peppers	2	2
Large yellow peppers	2	2
Water	²/₃ cup	150 mL
Cornstarch	2 tsp.	10 mL
Cooking oil	¹/₄ cup	60 mL
Garlic powder (or 2 cloves, minced)	¹/₂ tsp.	2 mL
Salt	¹/₄ tsp.	1 mL
Pepper	¹/₈ tsp.	0.5 mL

Arrange peppers on broiler pan, turning frequently, until skin is blistered and blackened. Remove peppers to bowl. Cover with plastic wrap. Let stand for 20 minutes. Remove skin and seeds, reserving juices. Cut into 1 inch (2.5 cm) squares. Turn into medium bowl. Strain juices into bowl.

Stir water into cornstarch in small saucepan. Add cooking oil, garlic powder, salt and pepper. Heat, stirring constantly, until boiling and slightly thickened. Pour over peppers. Stir. Cover. Chill for 24 hours. Makes 2¹/₂ to 3 cups (625 to 750 mL).

¹/₃ cup (75 mL): 52 Calories; 3.8 g Total Fat; 91 mg Sodium; 1 g Protein; 5 g Carbohydrate; 1 g Dietary Fiber

Pictured on page 108.

Prep Time: 30 minutes to roast peppers; 20 minutes to cool; 24 hours to chill.

To Make Ahead: Must be assembled at least 24 hours before serving. Cover. Keeps in the refrigerator for up to 3 days. Do not freeze.

Paré Pointer

If you cross a mink and a kangaroo you would have a fur coat with great big pockets.

Party Salad

A beautiful, glimmering salad, especially when served on
a dark plate. Unusual but interesting flavors.

Boiling water	³/₄ cup	175 mL
Packages raspberry-flavored gelatin (jelly powder), 3 oz. (85 g) each	2	2
Cans of stewed tomatoes (14 oz., 398 mL, each), with juice, broken up	2	2
Prepared orange (or other fruit) juice	2 tbsp.	30 mL
Drops of hot pepper sauce	4-6	4-6
SAUCE		
Light sour cream	1¹/₂ cups	375 mL
Prepared horseradish	2 tsp.	10 mL
Granulated sugar	¹/₂ tsp.	2 mL
Salt	¹/₈ tsp.	0.5 mL

Stir boiling water into jelly powder in large bowl until dissolved.

Add tomatoes with juice, orange juice and hot pepper sauce. Pour into 4¹/₂ to 5 cup (1.1 to 1.25 L) jelly mold. Chill at least 5 hours.

Sauce: Stir next 4 ingredients in small bowl. Unmold salad on large plate. Spoon or pipe sauce around bottom, completely surrounding salad. Makes 4¹/₂ cups (1.1 L).

¹/₃ cup (75 mL): 89 Calories; 2 g Total Fat; 235 mg Sodium; 3 g Protein; 17 g Carbohydrate; 1 g Dietary Fiber

Pictured on page 125.

Prep Time: 10 minutes.

To Make Ahead: Assemble early in day or night before. Cover and chill salad and sauce separately. Keeps in the refrigerator for up to 3 days.

 tip   *To make your shopping trip faster, group foods into categories of where they are found in your grocery store. This will save steps and time.*

Pickled Beet Salad

The whole salad turns a pretty pink from the beets.

Rotini pasta	6 oz.	170 g
Boiling water	1½ qts.	1.5 L
Salt	1½ tsp.	7 mL
Low-fat Italian dressing	½ cup	125 mL
Light salad dressing (or mayonnaise)	¼ cup	60 mL
Balsamic vinegar	1 tbsp.	15 mL
Granulated sugar	½ tsp.	2 mL
Salt	¼ tsp.	1 mL
Freshly ground pepper	¹⁄₁₆ tsp.	0.5 mL
White celery ribs (from center of stalk), thinly sliced (about 1 cup, 250 mL)	4	4
Medium carrot, very thinly sliced	1	1
Medium red onion, thinly sliced	½	½
Diced pickled beets, drained and blotted dry	1 cup	250 mL
Chopped fresh parsley, for garnish	3 tbsp.	50 mL

Cook pasta in boiling water and salt in large uncovered saucepan for 8 to 10 minutes until tender but firm. Drain. Rinse with cold water. Drain again.

Add next 6 ingredients to pasta. Toss. Stir in celery, carrot and red onion. Add beets. Toss.

Sprinkle with fresh parsley. Makes 6 cups (1.5 L).

¹⁄₃ cup (75 mL): 62 Calories; 1.3 g Total Fat; 209 mg Sodium; 1 g Protein; 11 g Carbohydrate; 1 g Dietary Fiber

Pictured on page 126.

Variation: Toss in 1 cup (250 mL) of diced cooked chicken or 6½ oz. (184 g) drained, flaked tuna if desired.

Prep Time: 15 minutes to prepare and assemble; 1 hour to chill.

To Make Ahead: Must be assembled at least 1 hour before serving but can also be assembled early in day. Cover. Chill. Keeps in the refrigerator for up to 2 days. Do not freeze.

Potato Cabbage Soup

A thick puréed soup enhanced with a sprinkling of cheese. Great flavor.

Margarine (or butter)	2 tbsp.	30 mL
Chopped onion	1 cup	250 mL
Cans of condensed chicken broth (10 oz., 284 mL, each)	2	2
Soup can of water	1	1
Grated cabbage	5 cups	1.25 L
Large potatoes, grated	2	2
Skim evaporated milk	½ cup	125 mL
Garlic powder (or 1 clove, minced)	¼ tsp.	1 mL
Salt, just a pinch		
Pepper, just a pinch		
Ground nutmeg	⅛ tsp.	0.5 mL
Ground marjoram	⅛ tsp.	0.5 mL
Water	2 tbsp.	30 mL
Cornstarch	1½ tsp.	7 mL
Grated light sharp Cheddar cheese	¾ cup	175 mL

Melt margarine in large pot or Dutch oven. Add onion. Sauté until soft.

Add chicken broth, first amount of water, cabbage and potato. Cook for about 20 minutes until cabbage is tender. Cool slightly then purée in blender. Return to pot.

Add next 6 ingredients. Heat, stirring often, until boiling.

Stir second amount of water into cornstarch in cup. Stir into soup until boiling and thickened.

Sprinkle individual servings with cheese. Makes 7 cups (1.75 L).

1 cup (250 mL): 164 Calories; 7 g Total Fat; 692 mg Sodium; 10 g Protein; 15 g Carbohydrate; 2 g Dietary Fiber

Pictured on page 72.

Prep Time: 20 minutes to prepare and assemble.

To Make Ahead: Prepare early in day or night before. Cover. Chill. To serve, reheat and garnish as above.

To Freeze: Divide among four 2 cup (500 mL) freezer containers (or size of choice). Label. Freeze for up to 3 months. To serve, heat from thawed or frozen state until hot. Garnish as above.

Bean Soup

So quick to prepare this robust soup using canned goods out of the cupboard.

Cooking oil	1 tbsp.	15 mL
Medium onions, chopped	2	2
Medium red pepper, chopped	1	1
Cans of diced tomatoes (14 oz., 398 mL, each), with juice	2	2
Cans of condensed beef broth (10 oz., 284 mL, each)	2	2
Can of beans in tomato sauce	14 oz.	398 mL
Can of pinto beans, drained	14 oz.	398 mL
Fancy (mild) molasses	2 tbsp.	30 mL
Chili powder	1 tbsp.	15 mL
Cayenne pepper	½ tsp.	2 mL
Ground allspice	¼ tsp.	1 mL

Heat cooking oil in large pot or Dutch oven. Add onion and red pepper. Sauté for about 3 minutes until soft.

Add remaining 8 ingredients. Stir. Bring to a boil. Cover. Simmer for about 1 hour, stirring occasionally. Makes 11 cups (2.75 L).

1 cup (250 mL): 120 Calories; 2.1 g Total Fat; 777 mg Sodium; 6 g Protein; 22 g Carbohydrate; 4 g Dietary Fiber

Pictured on page 72.

Prep Time: 15 to 20 minutes to prepare and assemble.

To Make Ahead: Prepare early in day or night before. Cover. Chill. To serve, reheat.

To Freeze: Divide among six 2 cup (500 mL) freezer containers (or size of choice). Freeze for up to 3 months. To serve, heat from thawed or frozen state until hot.

 Use Precut Veggies (onions and peppers), page 39, to make the preparation of this soup even quicker.

Minestrone Soup

Tender beef chunks in a thick meal-like soup.

Stew beef, cut into ½ inch (12 mm) cubes or smaller	1½ lbs.	680 g
Cooking oil	2 tsp.	10 mL
Cans of stewed tomatoes (14 oz., 398 mL, each)	2	2
Water	5 cups	1.25 L
Chopped celery	½ cup	125 mL
Chopped onion	½ cup	125 mL
Seasoned salt	2 tsp.	10 mL
Salt	2 tsp.	10 mL
Pepper	¼ tsp.	1 mL
Granulated sugar	1 tsp.	5 mL
Dried whole oregano	1¼ tsp.	6 mL
Dried sweet basil	1¼ tsp.	6 mL
Hot pepper sauce	¼-½ tsp.	1-2 mL
Beef bouillon powder (or liquid bouillon)	1½ tsp.	7 mL
Can of kidney beans, with liquid	14 oz.	398 mL
Sliced or diced zucchini, with peel	1 cup	250 mL
Broken short spaghetti pieces	1 cup	250 mL
Frozen peas	2 cups	500 mL

Grated light Parmesan cheese, for garnish

Brown beef in cooking oil in large pot or Dutch oven. Add next 12 ingredients. Stir. Bring to a boil. Cover. Simmer for 2 hours.

Add kidney beans, zucchini, spaghetti and peas. Stir. Bring to a boil. Simmer for 5 minutes until pasta is tender.

Sprinkle individual servings with cheese. Makes 13⅔ cups (3.4 L).

1 cup (250 mL): 191 Calories; 5.8 g Total Fat; 1027 mg Sodium; 16 g Protein; 19 g Carbohydrate; 4 g Dietary Fiber

Prep Time: 25 minutes to prepare and assemble.

To Make Ahead: Prepare early in day or night before. Cover. Chill. To serve, reheat.

To Freeze: Divide among seven 2 cup (500 mL) freezer containers (or size of choice). Freeze for up to 3 months. To serve, heat from thawed or frozen state until hot. Garnish as above.

Twice-Baked Potatoes

Creamy filling is a perfect piping consistency if you want to make these fancy for guests. Perfect to have on hand.

Medium potatoes (see Note)	6	6
Margarine (or butter)	2 tbsp.	30 mL
Light mayonnaise (not salad dressing)	½ cup	125 mL
Hot milk	½ cup	125 mL
Powdered Cheddar cheese product	¼ cup	60 mL
Parsley flakes	1 tsp.	5 mL
Onion salt	½ tsp.	2 mL
Seasoned salt	½ tsp.	2 mL
Pepper	⅛ tsp.	0.5 mL

Chopped chives, for garnish
Chopped green onion, for garnish
Grated Cheddar cheese, for garnish

Pierce potatoes in several spots. Place on rack in 400°F (205°C) oven for 50 to 60 minutes until tender. To test for doneness, insert sharp paring knife into center. Cool until able to handle. Cut potatoes in half lengthwise. Scoop out pulp into medium bowl, leaving thin coating on skins to form shell.

Add next 8 ingredients to potato pulp. Mash well. Stuff shells. Bake in 350°F (175°C) oven for 25 to 30 minutes to heat through.

Garnish with chives, green onion and a light sprinkle of cheese just before serving. Makes 12 stuffed potatoes.

1 stuffed potato: 144 Calories; 5.9 g Total Fat; 252 mg Sodium; 3 g Protein; 21 g Carbohydrate; 2 g Dietary Fiber

Pictured on page 143.

Note: For soft skins, wrap potatoes in foil or rub skin with cooking oil before placing in oven.

Prep Time: 30 minutes to prepare and assemble.

To Make Ahead: Prepare and stuff potatoes early in day or night before. Cover. Chill. To serve, bake as above.

To Freeze: Place stuffed potatoes on baking sheet. Freeze for 1 hour. Wrap partially frozen potatoes individually in foil. Freeze for up to 4 months. To serve, thaw and heat wrapped potatoes in 350°F (175°C) oven for 25 to 30 minutes until heated through.

Select-A-Meal: See page 12.

Oven Fries

These are so easy with the seasoning mix already prepared.
Try them dipped in light or non-fat sour cream.

SEASONING MIX

Salt	2 tsp.	10 mL
Seasoned salt	2 tsp.	10 mL
Pepper	1 tsp.	5 mL
Cayenne pepper	1/4 tsp.	1 mL
Paprika	2 tsp.	10 mL
Garlic powder	2 tsp.	10 mL
Grated Parmesan cheese	1/2 cup	125 mL
Parsley flakes	1 tbsp.	15 mL
Corn flake crumbs, finely crushed	1/2 cup	125 mL

Cooking oil, per potato (use about 1/2 tbsp.,
   7 mL, per medium potato)

Unpeeled medium potatoes, cut
   lengthwise into 8 wedges

Seasoning Mix: Combine first 9 ingredients in small bowl. Makes 1 1/3 cups (325 mL) seasoning, enough for about 42 potatoes.

Put 1/2 tbsp. (7 mL) cooking oil for each potato used into appropriate size bowl. Toss potato wedges in cooking oil to coat.

Sprinkle 1/2 tbsp. (7 mL) mix for each potato used over potatoes in bowl. Toss and stir until seasoning is evenly coated on wedges. Place on greased baking sheet or in foil-lined pan. Bake in 375°F (190°C) oven for 30 to 35 minutes.

1 serving: 137 Calories; 5.6 g Total Fat; 180 mg Sodium; 3 g Protein; 20 g Carbohydrate; 2 g Dietary Fiber

Pictured on front cover.

Prep Time: 5 minutes to prepare mix; 15 minutes to prepare 8 potatoes.

To Make Ahead: Prepare seasoning mix. Put into airtight container. Label. Store in refrigerator indefinitely. Do not freeze.

Cream Cheese Potatoes

Goes great with Chicken Pecan, page 79.

Medium potatoes, cut up	8	8
Boiling water		
Light cream cheese, softened	8 oz.	250 g
Light sour cream (or plain yogurt or mayonnaise)	1/3 cup	75 mL
Milk	1/2 cup	125 mL
Salt	1/2 tsp.	2 mL
Pepper	1/4 tsp.	1 mL
Paprika	1/2 tsp.	2 mL
Margarine (or butter), optional		

Cook potato in boiling water in large saucepan until tender. Drain. Mash.

Cut up cream cheese. Add to potato. Add sour cream, milk, salt and pepper. Mash well. Beat until fluffy. Turn into ungreased 2 quart (2 L) casserole. Sprinkle with paprika.

Make indentations in surface and dot with margarine. Cover. Bake in 325°F (160°C) oven for about 30 minutes. Serves 8.

1 serving: 191 Calories; 5.7 g Total Fat; 457 mg Sodium; 6 g Protein; 29 g Carbohydrate; 2 g Dietary Fiber

Prep Time: 20 minutes to prepare and assemble.

To Make Ahead: Assemble early in day or night before. Cover. Chill. To serve, dot with margarine and bake as above.

To Freeze: Tightly cover unbaked casserole with foil. Label. Freeze for up to 3 months. To serve, thaw and reheat as above. Texture will be watery until hot. Once hot, up to 1/2 cup (125 mL) milk may be needed to restore creamy texture.

Select-A-Meal: See page 12.

Paré Pointer

Definition of fascinate: Two of my ten buttons came off my shirt so I could only fasten eight.

Mashed Potatoes Select

These are made delicious with the addition of sour cream.
They freeze and reheat beautifully.

Medium potatoes, cut into chunks	5 lbs.	2.3 kg
Boiling water, to cover		
Salt	1 tsp.	5 mL
Light sour cream	²/₃ cup	150 mL
Milk	½ cup	125 mL
Seasoned salt	½ tsp.	2 mL
Onion salt	¼ tsp.	1 mL
Pepper	⅛ tsp.	0.5 mL

Cook potato in boiling water and salt in large saucepan until tender. Drain. Mash.

Add remaining 5 ingredients. Mash well. To make very fluffy, beat with electric beater. Spread in greased 3 quart (3 L) casserole. Cover. Heat in 350°F (175°C) oven for about 45 minutes until heated through, stirring at half-time. Makes 11 cups (2.75 L).

1 cup (250 mL): 184 Calories; 1.4 g Total Fat; 360 mg Sodium; 4 g Protein; 40 g Carbohydrate; 3 g Dietary Fiber

Pictured on page 126.

Prep Time: 15 minutes.

To Make Ahead: Prepare early in day or night before. Chill. To serve, bake as above.

To Freeze: Divide potato mixture among five 2 cup (500 mL) freezer containers (or size of choice). Label. Freeze for up to 3 months. To serve, thaw and bake smaller amounts as above for about 15 minutes. See Tip, page 148. To bake from frozen state, heat smaller amount in 350°F (175°C) oven for about 50 minutes. Fluff with fork.

Select-A-Meal: See page 12.

Broccoli Bake

Looks as appealing as it tastes—a wonderful dish for company.

Frozen broccoli, thawed and drained	15 oz.	500 g
Can of tomatoes, drained	14 oz.	398 mL
Light mayonnaise (not salad dressing)	1¼ cups	300 mL
Grated light Parmesan cheese	½ cup	125 mL
Grated light Parmesan cheese	2 tbsp.	30 mL

(continued on next page)

Arrange broccoli in greased 2 quart (2 L) casserole. Break up tomatoes. Drain again. Spread over broccoli.

Mix mayonnaise and first amount of cheese. Spoon randomly over tomatoes. Spread.

Sprinkle with second amount of cheese. Bake, uncovered, in 325°F (160°C) oven for about 50 minutes. Serves 6.

1 serving: 225 Calories; 18 g Total Fat; 643 mg Sodium; 7 g Protein; 11 g Carbohydrate; 3 g Dietary Fiber

Prep Time: 10 minutes to prepare and assemble.

To Make Ahead: Assemble early in day or night before. Cover. Chill. To serve, bake as above. Do not freeze.

Glazed Carrots

You'll even have the children asking for more of these orange-sauced carrots.

Carrots, cut into small chunks or coins	1 lb.	454 g
Boiling water, to cover		
Hard margarine (or butter), melted	2 tbsp.	30 mL
Liquid honey	1 tbsp.	15 mL
Frozen concentrated orange juice	2 tbsp.	30 mL
(or 2 tsp., 10 mL, grated orange peel)		
Salt, just a pinch		

Cook carrot in boiling water in medium saucepan until tender. Drain well.

Mix margarine, honey, orange juice and salt in cup. Add to carrot. Toss to coat. Serves 4.

1 serving: 132 Calories; 5.8 g Total Fat; 141 mg Sodium; 2 g Protein; 20 g Carbohydrate; 3 g Dietary Fiber

Pictured on page 144.

Prep Time: 25 minutes to prepare and assemble.

To Make Ahead: Peel and cut carrots and prepare glaze early in day or night before. Cover and chill separately. To serve, cook carrot as above. Toss with glaze. Do not freeze.

Baked Onions

They open like a flower while baking. Makes economical use of oven while heating main dish.

Medium onions	6	6
Hard margarine (or butter)	6 tsp.	30 mL
Brown sugar, packed	6 tsp.	30 mL
Salt, sprinkle		
Pepper, sprinkle		

Remove onion skin. Place each onion on foil square. Cut down from top to almost 1 inch (2.5 cm) from bottom. Spread apart a bit and insert 1 tsp. (5 mL) each of margarine and brown sugar. Sprinkle with salt and pepper. Draw foil to top and scrunch together. Put wrapped onions in 9 x 13 inch (22 x 33 cm) pan. Bake in 350°F (175°C) oven for 1 to 1½ hours until tender. Serves 6.

1 serving: 96 Calories; 4.1 g Total Fat; 51 mg Sodium; 1 g Protein; 14 g Carbohydrate; 2 g Dietary Fiber

Prep Time: 15 minutes to assemble.

To Make Ahead: Assemble early in day or night before. Chill. To serve, bake as above. Do not freeze.

Green Beans Deluxe

A simple dish. Just enough sauce to coat the beans and a crunchy topping to finish them off.

Frozen french-cut green beans	2.2 lbs.	1 kg
Sliced fresh mushrooms	1 cup	250 mL
Boiling water		
Can of condensed cream of mushroom soup	10 oz.	284 mL
Can of french-fried onion rings	2¾ oz.	79 g

Cook beans and mushrooms in boiling water in large saucepan for 2 to 3 minutes until tender-crisp. Drain. Transfer to ungreased 3 quart (3 L) casserole.

(continued on next page)

Empty soup into medium bowl. Stir vigorously. Spoon over top of vegetables. Scatter onion rings over top. Bake, uncovered, in 350°F (175°C) oven for 25 to 35 minutes until heated through. Serves 8.

1 serving: 106 Calories; 4.9 g Total Fat; 373 mg Sodium; 3 g Protein; 15 g Carbohydrate; 3 g Dietary Fiber

Prep Time: 15 minutes to prepare and assemble.

To Make Ahead: Assemble early in day or night before. Cover. Chill. To serve, bake as above. Do not freeze.

Baked Corn

A triple dose of corn flavor in this rich and hearty casserole. Goes a long way to serve 8 as a side dish.

Can of cream-style corn	14 oz.	398 mL
Can of kernel corn, drained	12 oz.	341 mL
Light sour cream	1 cup	250 mL
Margarine (or butter), melted	¼ cup	60 mL
All-purpose flour	1 cup	250 mL
Yellow cornmeal	⅔ cup	150 mL
Granulated sugar	2 tbsp.	30 mL
Baking powder	1 tbsp.	15 mL
Salt	¼ tsp.	1 mL

Stir first 4 ingredients together in medium bowl.

Combine remaining 5 ingredients in large bowl. Add corn mixture. Stir just to moisten. Turn into ungreased 2 quart (2 L) casserole. Bake, uncovered, in 375°F (190°C) oven for about 1 hour until crusty-brown on top. Serves 8.

1 serving: 259 Calories; 8.5 g Total Fat; 406 mg Sodium; 5 g Protein; 43 g Carbohydrate; 2 g Dietary Fiber

Prep Time: 10 minutes to prepare and assemble.

To Make Ahead: Prepare early in day or night before. Cover and chill corn mixture. Store flour mixture in airtight container at room temperature. To serve, assemble and bake as above. Do not freeze.

 tip *The flour mixture in the above recipe can be stored for up to 12 months in an airtight container in the cupboard.*

Really Lazy Holubchi

This is quick and easy.

Long grain white rice, uncooked	1½ cups	375 mL
Finely chopped onion	1 cup	250 mL
Can of stewed tomatoes, with juice	14 oz.	398 mL
Bacon slices, cooked crisp and crumbled	3	3
Small head of cabbage (or ½ medium)	5 cups	1.25 L
Granulated sugar	½ tsp.	2 mL
Salt	1 tsp.	5 mL
Pepper	¼ tsp.	1 mL
Can of tomato juice	19 oz.	540 mL

Stir all 9 ingredients together in large bowl. Turn into greased 3 quart (3 L) casserole. Cover. Bake in 350°F (175°C) oven for about 1 hour. Remove cover. Bake for 30 minutes, stirring at half-time. Makes 8 cups (2 L), enough for 8 servings.

1 serving: 188 Calories; 1.3 g Total Fat; 755 mg Sodium; 5 g Protein; 40 g Carbohydrate; 3 g Dietary Fiber

Prep Time: 30 minutes to prepare and assemble.

To Make Ahead: Assemble early in day or night before. Cover. Chill. To serve, bake as above.

To Freeze: Bake, cool and cover. Label. Freeze for up to 2 months. To serve, thaw and heat, uncovered, in 350°F (175°C) oven until hot. To bake from frozen state, see Tip, page 69.

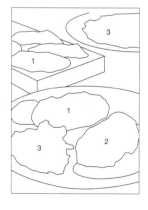

1. Twice-Baked Potatoes, page 135
2. Ham Loaves, page 117
3. Cheesy Green Salad, page 123

Props Courtesy Of: Stokes
The Bay

Green Rice

Delicate onion and spinach flavors.

Long grain white rice	2 cups	500 mL
Chopped onion	1½ cups	375 mL
Chicken bouillon powder	1½ tbsp.	25 mL
Water	4 cups	1 L
Large eggs	2	2
Frozen chopped spinach, thawed, squeezed dry and chopped more	10 oz.	300 g
Seasoned salt	½ tsp.	2 mL
Salt	½ tsp.	2 mL
Pepper	¼ tsp.	1 mL

Combine rice, onion, bouillon powder and water in large saucepan. Bring to a boil. Simmer for 15 to 20 minutes on low until tender and liquid is absorbed. Remove from heat. Cool slightly.

Beat eggs in small bowl until smooth. Add spinach, seasoned salt, salt and pepper. Mix well. Stir gently into rice. Bake, uncovered, in 350°F (175°C) oven for about 15 minutes. A knife inserted off center should come out clean. Makes 8 cups (2 L).

1 cup (250 mL): 220 Calories; 2 g Total Fat; 661 mg Sodium; 6 g Protein; 43 g Carbohydrate; 2 g Dietary Fiber

Pictured on page 144.

Prep Time: 10 minutes to assemble (plus 40 minutes cooking time).

To Make Ahead: Assemble early in day or night before. To serve, bake as above.

To Freeze: Divide baked casserole among four 2 cup (500 mL) containers (or size of choice). Label. Freeze for up to 2 months. To serve, thaw, cover and reheat.

Select-A-Meal: See page 12.

1. Green Rice, above
2. Glazed Carrots, page 139
3. Cordon Bleu Roll, page 78

Butter Baked Rice

Excellent flavor with fluffy texture. Makes economical
use of oven when cooked with main course.

Long grain white rice	1 cup	250 mL
Salt	1 tsp.	5 mL
Boiling water, to cover		
Butter (or margarine)	⅓ cup	75 mL
Garlic salt, sprinkle		
Chicken stock (or 2 cups, 500 mL, boiling water and 2 tsp., 10 mL, chicken bouillon powder)	2 cups	500 mL
Chopped fresh parsley	3 tbsp.	50 mL
Slivered almonds	¼ cup	60 mL
Chopped fresh parsley	1 tbsp.	15 mL

Measure rice and salt into small bowl. Cover with boiling water. Let stand for 30 minutes. Drain through strainer. Rinse with cold water. Drain.

Melt butter in frying pan. Add rice. Sauté for about 5 minutes, stirring often, until butter is mostly absorbed. Transfer to ungreased 1 quart (1 L) casserole.

Sprinkle with garlic salt. Pour chicken stock over top. Cover. Bake in 350°F (175°C) oven for about 1 hour.

Add first amount of parsley and fluff with fork. Sprinkle with almonds and second amount of parsley. Bake for 5 minutes. Make 3 cups (750 mL). Serves 4.

1 serving: 398 Calories; 22 g Total Fat; 1057 mg Sodium; 8 g Protein; 42 g Carbohydrate; 1 g Dietary Fiber

---

Prep Time: 15 minutes to prepare and assemble (plus 30 minutes stand time).

To Make Ahead: Assemble in casserole early in day or night before. Cover. Chill. To serve, bake as above.

To Freeze: Double or triple the recipe. Divide baked casserole among 1½ cup (375 mL) freezer containers (or size of choice). Label. Freeze for up to 3 months. To serve, thaw and reheat.

Select-A-Meal: See page 12.

Bread Stuffing

A perfect blend of herb flavors makes this a delicious accompaniment.

Cooking oil	2 tsp.	10 mL
Chopped onion	1 cup	250 mL
Coarse dry bread crumbs	4 cups	1 L
Chicken bouillon powder	2 tsp.	10 mL
Parsley flakes	2 tsp.	10 mL
Poultry seasoning	2 tsp.	10 mL
Celery salt	⅛ tsp.	0.5 mL
Salt	¼ tsp.	1 mL
Pepper	¼ tsp.	1 mL
Hot water	¼ cup	60 mL
Margarine (or butter), melted	2 tbsp.	30 mL

Heat cooking oil in frying pan. Add onion. Sauté until soft and clear.

Measure bread crumbs into large bowl. Add bouillon powder, parsley, poultry seasoning, celery salt, salt and pepper. Stir well. Add onion. Mix.

Add hot water, 1 tbsp. (15 mL) at a time, and melted margarine, tossing well until desired consistency. Add more or less water as desired. Makes 3 cups (750 mL).

½ cup (125 mL): 362 Calories; 8.9 g Total Fat; 175 mg Sodium; 10 g Protein; 59 g Carbohydrate; 2 g Dietary Fiber

Pictured on page 126.

Prep Time: 20 minutes.

To Make Ahead: Prepare early in day or night before. Cool. Cover. Chill. To serve, reheat.

To Freeze: Make several recipes. Divide among 2 cup (500 mL) freezer containers (or size of choice). Label. Freeze for up to 3 months. To serve, thaw, cover and reheat.

Select-A-Meal: See page 12.

Paré Pointer

He wasn't happy to find some hairs in his rabbit stew.

Sweetened Butternut Squash

When there's an abundance of squash in the garden,
make up this recipe to have on hand for later. Other squash,
such as Hubbard and Acorn, can be used but the texture and color
may vary accordingly. Use in Squash And Beef Pie, page 21.

Butternut squash, cut in half	3 lbs.	1.4 kg
Boiling water	¼ cup	60 mL
Brown sugar, packed	1½ tsp.	7 mL
Salt	¼ tsp.	1 mL
Pepper, just a pinch		
Hard margarine (or butter), optional, cut into 6 pieces	1 tbsp.	15 mL

Remove seeds from squash. Place, cut side down, in ungreased 9 x 13 inch (22 x 33 cm) pan. Add boiling water. Cover with foil. Bake in 350°F (175°C) oven for 1 hour until flesh is tender. Remove flesh with spoon to large bowl. Discard shells.

Add brown sugar, salt and pepper. Mash well. Turn into small ungreased casserole. Make 6 indentations in top. Place about ½ tsp. (2 mL) margarine in each cavity. Cover. Bake in 350°F (175°C) oven for 30 minutes until hot. Makes total of 4 cups (1 L).

1 cup (250 mL): 96 Calories; 0.6 g Total Fat; 180 mg Sodium; 4 g Protein; 23 g Carbohydrate; 4 g Dietary Fiber

Prep Time: 5 minutes to remove seeds.

To Make Ahead: Assemble in casserole early in day or night before. Cover. Chill. To serve, bake as above.

To Freeze: Divide between two 2 cup (500 mL) freezer containers (or size of choice). Label. Freeze for up to 3 months. To serve, thaw, cover and reheat. See Tip, below.

Select-A-Meal: See page 12.

To shorten the cooking time of a frozen casserole, defrost in the microwave first. Generally, 8 minutes per pound (454 g) on defrost (30%) is sufficient.

Vegetables

Parsnip Bake

There's a lovely orange background to these slightly sweet parsnips.
Makes lots for company.

Parsnips, sliced into 1 inch (2.5 cm) coins	2.2 lbs.	1 kg
Boiling water		
Salt		
Brown sugar, packed	⅓ cup	75 mL
Prepared orange juice	⅓ cup	75 mL
Margarine (or butter), optional,	1 tbsp.	15 mL
cut into 6 pieces		
Salt, sprinkle		
Pepper, sprinkle		

Cook parsnip in boiling water and salt in large saucepan until tender. Drain. Mash.

Add brown sugar and orange juice. Mash well. Turn into ungreased 2 quart (2 L) casserole. Make 6 indentations in top. Place about ½ tsp. (2 mL) margarine in each. Sprinkle with salt and pepper. Cover. Bake in 350°F (175°C) oven for 30 minutes until hot. Makes 6 cups (1.5 L).

½ cup (125 mL): 92 Calories; 0.3 g Total Fat; 339 mg Sodium; 1 g Protein; 23 g Carbohydrate; 3 g Dietary Fiber

Prep Time: 20 minutes to prepare and assemble.

To Make Ahead: Assemble in casserole early in day or night before. Cover. Chill. To serve, bake as above.

To Freeze: Divide among three 2 cup (500 mL) freezer containers (or size of choice). Label. Freeze for up to 3 months. To serve, thaw, cover and reheat. See Tip, page 148.

Select-A-Meal: See page 12.

Paré Pointer
Combine a centipede and a parrot and you will get a walkie-talkie.

Dressed Cauliflower

Creamy and tangy sauce with a touch of curry
to complement the cauliflower. Exceptionally good.

Medium head of cauliflower (about 2 lbs., 900 g), broken into florets	1	1
All-purpose flour	3 tbsp.	50 mL
Chicken bouillon powder	1 tsp.	5 mL
Curry powder	1 tsp.	5 mL
Onion powder	1/4 tsp.	1 mL
Salt	1/4 tsp.	1 mL
Milk	1 1/2 cups	375 mL
Light salad dressing (or mayonnaise)	1/3 cup	75 mL
Grated light sharp Cheddar cheese	1 cup	250 mL
Margarine (or butter)	2 tbsp.	30 mL
Dry bread crumbs	1/2 cup	125 mL

Place cauliflower pieces in ungreased 2 quart (2 L) casserole.

Stir flour, bouillon powder, curry, onion powder and salt in medium saucepan. Whisk in milk gradually until no lumps remain. Heat, stirring continually, until boiling and thickened. Remove from heat.

Add salad dressing and cheese. Stir well. Pour over cauliflower. Stir gently until sauce is well distributed.

Melt margarine in small saucepan. Add bread crumbs. Mix well. Sprinkle over casserole. Bake, uncovered, in 350°F (175°C) oven for about 60 minutes until cauliflower is tender. Serves 6.

1 serving: 257 Calories; 13 g Total Fat; 629 mg Sodium; 12 g Protein; 24 g Carbohydrate; 3 g Dietary Fiber

Prep Time: 30 minutes to prepare and assemble.

To Make Ahead: Assemble in casserole early in day or night before. Cover. Chill. To serve, bake as above. Do not freeze as cauliflower will be too watery.

Measurement Tables

Throughout this book measurements are given in Conventional and Metric measure. To compensate for differences between the two measurements due to rounding, a full metric measure is not always used. The cup used is the standard 8 fluid ounce. Temperature is given in degrees Fahrenheit and Celsius. Baking pan measurements are in inches and centimetres as well as quarts and litres. An exact metric conversion is given below as well as the working equivalent (Standard Measure).

Spoons

Conventional Measure	Metric Exact Conversion Millilitre (mL)	Metric Standard Measure Millilitre (mL)
1/8 teaspoon (tsp.)	0.6 mL	0.5 mL
1/4 teaspoon (tsp.)	1.2 mL	1 mL
1/2 teaspoon (tsp.)	2.4 mL	2 mL
1 teaspoon (tsp.)	4.7 mL	5 mL
2 teaspoons (tsp.)	9.4 mL	10 mL
1 tablespoon (tbsp.)	14.2 mL	15 mL

Cups

Conventional Measure	Metric Exact Conversion Millilitre (mL)	Metric Standard Measure Millilitre (mL)
1/4 cup (4 tbsp.)	56.8 mL	60 mL
1/3 cup (51/3 tbsp.)	75.6 mL	75 mL
1/2 cup (8 tbsp.)	113.7 mL	125 mL
2/3 cup (102/3 tbsp.)	151.2 mL	150 mL
3/4 cup (12 tbsp.)	170.5 mL	175 mL
1 cup (16 tbsp.)	227.3 mL	250 mL
41/2 cups	1022.9 mL	1000 mL (1 L)

Oven Temperatures

Fahrenheit (°F)	Celsius (°C)
175°	80°
200°	95°
225°	110°
250°	120°
275°	140°
300°	150°
325°	160°
350°	175°
375°	190°
400°	205°
425°	220°
450°	230°
475°	240°
500°	260°

Dry Measurements

Conventional Measure Ounces (oz.)	Metric Exact Conversion Grams (g)	Metric Standard Measure Grams (g)
1 oz.	28.3 g	28 g
2 oz.	56.7 g	57 g
3 oz.	85.0 g	85 g
4 oz.	113.4 g	125 g
5 oz.	141.7 g	140 g
6 oz.	170.1 g	170 g
7 oz.	198.4 g	200 g
8 oz.	226.8 g	250 g
16 oz.	453.6 g	500 g
32 oz.	907.2 g	1000 g (1 kg)

Pans

Conventional Inches	Metric Centimetres
x8 inch	20x20 cm
x9 inch	22x22 cm
x13 inch	22x33 cm
0x15 inch	25x38 cm
1x17 inch	28x43 cm
x2 inch round	20x5 cm
x2 inch round	22x5 cm
0x41/2 inch tube	25x11 cm
x4x3 inch loaf	20x10x7.5 cm
x5x3 inch loaf	22x12.5x7.5 cm

Casseroles

CANADA & BRITAIN Standard Size Casserole	Exact Metric Measure	UNITED STATES Standard Size Casserole	Exact Metric Measure
1 qt. (5 cups)	1.13 L	1 qt. (5 cups)	900 mL
11/2 qts. (71/2 cups)	1.69 L	11/2 qts. (71/2 cups)	1.35 L
2 qts. (10 cups)	2.25 L	2 qts. (10 cups)	1.8 L
21/2 qts. (121/2 cups)	2.81 L	21/2 qts. (121/2 cups)	2.25 L
3 qts. (15 cups)	3.38 L	3 qts. (15 cups)	2.7 L
4 qts. (20 cups)	4.5 L	4 qts. (20 cups)	3.6 L
5 qts. (25 cups)	5.63 L	5 qts. (25 cups)	4.5 L

151

Index

154

Photo Index

Tip Index

Feature Recipe from

Chocolate Everything

No food stimulates our senses so completely. No flavor evokes such a feeling of joy and abandon. No texture is so smooth and refined as chocolate...if not an addiction, then certainly a passion!

Mini Chip Cheesecakes

Smooth and creamy with lots of little chocolate bits. Garnish with whipped topping and Chocolate Filigrees, page 24, just before serving.

Chocolate wafers	12	12
Light cream cheese (8 oz., 250 g, each), softened	2	2
Granulated sugar	¾ cup	175 mL
Large eggs	2	2
Vanilla	1 tsp.	5 mL
Mini semisweet chocolate chips	½ cup	125 mL
Mini semisweet chocolate chips	½ cup	125 mL

Line ungreased muffin cups with large paper liners. Place 1 wafer in bottom of each liner.

Beat cream cheese and sugar in medium bowl until smooth. Beat in eggs, 1 at a time, on low just until blended. Add vanilla. Mix in.

Melt first amount of chocolate chips in small saucepan over hot water, or on low, stirring constantly, until smooth. Do not overheat. Add to batter.

Add second amount of chocolate chips. Fold in. Divide over wafers. Bake in 325°F (160°C) oven for 25 to 30 minutes until set. Cool, then chill. Makes 12.

1 cheesecake: 275 Calories; 7 g Protein; 15.2 g Total Fat; 31 g Carbohydrate; 462 mg Sodium; 1 g Dietary Fiber

Company's Coming cookbooks are available at retail locations **throughout** Canada!

See mail order form

Buy any 2 cookbooks—choose a 3rd FREE of equal or less value than the lowest price paid.   *Available in French

Assorted Titles

CODE		
BE	Beef Today! (softcover)	CA$19.99 Canada US$15.99 USA & International
KLU	Kids-Lunches	CA$14.99 Canada US$10.99 USA & International

Special Occasion Series   CA$19.99 Canada

CODE		
CE	Chocolate Everything* **NEW** October 2000	US$19.99 USA & International
EE	Easy Entertaining* (hardcover)	US$19.99 USA & International

Lifestyle Series   CA$16.99 Canada   US$12.99 USA & International

CODE		CODE		CODE	
GR	Grilling* **NEW**	LFC	Low-fat Cooking*	LFP	Low-fat Pasta*

Original Series   CA$14.99 Canada   US$10.99 USA & International

CODE		CODE		CODE	
SQ	150 Delicious Squares*	DI	Dinners of the World	MU	Muffins & More*
AP	Appetizers	FS	Fish & Seafood*	ODM	One-Dish Meals*
BA	Barbecues*	HE	Holiday Entertaining*	PA	Pasta*
BR	Breads*	KC	Kids Cooking*	PI	Pies*
BB	Breakfasts & Brunches*	LCA	Light Casseroles*	PZ	Pizza!*
CK	Cakes	LR	Light Recipes*	PR	Preserves*
CA	Casseroles*	LU	Lunches*	SA	Salads*
CH	Chicken, Etc.*	MC	Main Courses	SC	Slow Cooker Recipes
CO	Cookies*	MAM	Make-Ahead Meals* **NEW**	SS	Soups & Sandwiches
CT	Cooking For Two*	ME	Meatless Cooking*	ST	Starters*
DE	Desserts	MI	Microwave Cooking*	SF	Stir-Fry*
				VE	Vegetables

Greatest Hits   CA$12.99 Canada   US$9.99 USA & International

CODE		CODE	
BML	Biscuits, Muffins & Loaves*	SAW	Sandwiches & Wraps* **NEW**
DSD	Dips, Spreads & Dressings*	SAS	Soups & Salads* **NEW**

Select Series   CA$10.99 Canada   US$7.99 USA & International

CODE		CODE	
B&R	Beans & Rice*	NBD	No-Bake Desserts
MAS	Make-Ahead Salads	S&M	Sauces & Marinades*

Company's Coming
COOKBOOKS ®

www.**company**scoming.com
visit our ↖web-site

COMPANY'S COMING PUBLISHING LIMITED
2311 - 96 Street
Edmonton, Alberta, Canada T6N 1G3
Tel: (780) 450-6223 Fax: (780) 450-1857

Exclusive Mail Order Offer

See page 158 for list of cookbooks

Buy **2** Get **1** FREE!

Buy any 2 cookbooks—choose a **3rd FREE** of equal or less value than the lowest price paid.

Quantity	Code	Title	Price Each	Price Total
			$	$
		don't forget		
		to indicate your		
		free book(s).		
		(see exclusive mail order		
		offer above)		
		please print		

TOTAL BOOKS (including FREE)	**TOTAL BOOKS PURCHASED:** $

	International	Canada & USA
Plus Shipping & Handling (per destination)	**$7.00** (one book)	**$5.00** (1-3 books)
Additional Books (including FREE books)	$ ($2.00 each)	$ ($1.00 each)
Sub-Total	$	$
Canadian residents add G.S.T(7%)		$
TOTAL AMOUNT ENCLOSED	$	$

The Fine Print

- Orders outside Canada must be **PAID IN US FUNDS** by cheque or money order drawn on Canadian or US bank or by credit card.
- Make cheque or money order payable to: **COMPANY'S COMING PUBLISHING LIMITED.**
- Prices are expressed in Canadian dollars for Canada, US dollars for USA & International and are subject to change without prior notice.
- Orders are shipped surface mail. For courier rates, visit our web-site: **www.companyscoming.com** or contact us: **Tel: (780) 450-6223 Fax: (780) 450-1857.**
- Sorry, no C.O.D's.

Gift Giving

- Let us help you with your gift giving!
- We will send cookbooks directly to the recipients of your choice if you give us their names and addresses.
- Please specify the titles you wish to send to each person.
- If you would like to include your personal note or card, we will be pleased to enclose it with your gift order.
- Company's Coming Cookbooks make excellent gifts: Birthdays, bridal showers, Mother's Day, Father's Day, graduation or any occasion...collect them all!

☐ MasterCard   ☐ VISA

Expiry date _____

Account # _____

Name of cardholder _____

Cardholder's signature _____

Shipping Address

Send the cookbooks listed above to:

Name: _____

Street: _____

City: _____ Prov./State: _____

Country: _____ Postal Code/Zip: _____

Tel: (_____) _____

E-mail address: _____

YES! Please send a catalogue: ☐ English ☐ French

We'd love to hear from you

We welcome your comments and would love to hear from you. Please take a few moments to give us your feedback. Thank you.

How many meals in a week do you cook in your home? _____

How often do you refer to a cookbook (or other source) for recipes?

❑ Everyday ❑ Two or three times in a ❑ Once a month
❑ A few times a week   month ❑ A few times a year

What recipe features are most important to you? Rank 1 to 5; (1 being most important, 5 being least important).

_____ Recipes for everyday cooking using everyday ingredients

_____ Recipes for guests and entertaining

_____ Easy recipes; quick to prepare

_____ Low-fat or health related nutritional information

_____ Confidence in quality of recipe

What is most important about the content of a cookbook? Rank 1 to 5; (1 being most important, 5 being least important).

_____ Lots of color photographs of recipes

_____ How-to & instructional information

_____ Helpful hints & cooking tips

_____ Information on time spent for preparation

_____ Information on whether the recipe can be made ahead or frozen

What features do you find most important in a cookbook? Rank 1 to 5; (1 being most important, 5 being least important).

_____ Lay-flat binding (coil or cerlox)   _____ Well organized

_____ Hardcover   _____ Complete index

_____ Softcover

How many cookbooks have you purchased in the last year? _____
Of these, how many were gifts? _____

Age group

❑ Under 18 ❑ 25 to 34 ❑ 45 to 54 ❑ 65+
❑ 18 to 24 ❑ 35 to 44 ❑ 55 to 64

Additional comments about topics you would like Company's Coming to publish or things you like most about a cookbook.

_____

_____

_____

Thank you for sharing your views and opinions with us. Please mail or fax to:
Company's Coming Publishing Limited, 2311 - 96 Street,
Edmonton, Alberta, Canada T6N 1G3 Fax: (780) 450-1857

We're listening

MAM1